SUBMARINERS VC.

By the Same Author
ARK ROYAL
THE FLEET THAT JACK BUILT
Both available from Periscope Publishing

Submariners VC.

Fourteen men of the Royal Navy's Silent Service
who received the highest award for bravery

Rear-Admiral Sir William Jameson KBE. CB.

Periscope Publishing Ltd.
Penzance

First Published by Peter Davies in 1962

Republished in 2004 by
Periscope Publishing Ltd.
33 Barwis Terrace
Penzance
Cornwall TR18 2AW
www.periscopepublishing.com

A CIP record for this book is available from the
British Library

ISBN No 1-904381-24-3

Printed in England by Anthony Rowe Ltd,
Eastbourne

Contents

Illustrations

Photographs are inserted as a complete 12-page section between pages 96 and 97. Nos. 4 and 5 are reproduced by courtesy of the Wardroom Mess, H.M.S. *Dolphin*; No. 7a by courtesy of the *Daily Herald*; No. 7b by courtesy of Mr. Gould V.C.; and the remainder by courtesy of the Imperial War Museum.

Maps are included in the sections to which they first refer.

The sketch-map illustration of the attack on the *Tirpitz*, on page 175, is from the personal sketchbook of the late Commander Donald Cameron V.C., and is reproduced here by kind permission of his widow.

Acknowledgements

The patrol reports rendered by the Commanding Officers of submarines, written shortly after the events they describe from data entered in logs and notebooks at the time, are the basis for much of this book. I wish to express my gratitude to the Lord Commissioners of the Admiralty for making these reports, and other official documents, available to me, and to the Director of Publications, H.M. Stationery Office. For the French submarines mentioned in the early chapters I am indebted to Capitaine de Vaisseau R. Caroff of the Service Historique of the Ministère des Armées (Marine) who sent me extracts from *Le Livre d'Or de la Marine Française* (Guèrre 1914-1918). My work at the Admiralty was guided and facilitated by Messrs. F. H. Wilkinson, S. S. Bailey and E. F. J. Hooper of the Records Department, by Lieutenant Commander P. K. Kemp, the Admiralty Archivist and by Miss V. S. Heath of the Admiralty Library to all of whom my most grateful thanks are due. A great deal of supporting material was obtained from the library of the Imperial War Museum and I am much beholden to Miss R. Coombs, the librarian and to Mr. V. Rigby; also to the staff of the London Library and of H.M. Record Office.

It would be impracticable to mention all those who have helped me by searching their memories and supplying information, but I wish to record my special gratitude to Commander N. D. Holbrook V.C., Rear-Admiral E. Courtney Boyle V.C., Commander R. W. Lawrence D.S.C., Admiral Sir Martin Dunbar-Nasmith V.C., K.C.B., K.C.M.G., D.L., Mrs. D'Oyly-Hughes and her daughter Mrs. Riviere, Vice-Admiral Sir Sydney Raw K.B.E., C.B. the President of the Submarine Old Comrades Association, Mr. W. Briggs, Secretary of the Australian Branch of the

ACKNOWLEDGEMENTS

S.O.C.A., Mr. R. A. Perkins D.S.M., Mrs. Saxton White, Rear-Admiral G. W. G. Simpson C.B., C.B.E., Mr. John Cawte, for so many years the Wardroom Mess Secretary of H.M.S. *Dolphin*, Canon W. M. Lummis, M.C. that mine of information on those awarded the Victoria Cross, Mr. T. W. Gould V.C., Rear-Admiral Sir Anthony C. C. Miers V.C., K.B.E., C.B., D.S.O., Rear-Admiral H. S. Mackenzie D.S.O., D.S.C., Mrs. J. W. Linton, Captain J. A. R. Troup D.S.C., Mrs. D. Cameron, Captain B. C. G. Place V.C., D.S.C., Lady Barry and Lieutenant-Commander I. E. Fraser V.C., D.S.C., R.N.R.

I wish also to acknowledge the help I have received from an old submariner whom I have been unable to trace, Leading Stoker J. T. Haskins, who kept a diary during E 14's first patrol in the Sea of Marmara, extracts from which I have seen in the Imperial War Museum, and made use of.

Miss Margaret Dyson, late of the W.R.N.S., transformed my longhand into neat typescript. My wife, as usual, helped me in very many ways. Last, but certainly not least, I was most fortunate in having an old submariner, Mr. Alexander Fullerton of Peter Davies Ltd., to check my script and to give me valuable advice.

W. S. J.

Foreword

By Rear-Admiral G. W. G. Simpson, C.B., C.B.E.

Rear-Admiral Simpson became 'Commander Sub-marines Malta' in January 1941, and Captain of the famous 10th Submarine Flotilla when it was formed in September of that year. Before the Allied landings in North Africa he assumed operational command of all submarines in the Mediterranean. He left Malta in January 1943, when the siege was lifted after the 8th Army's capture of Tripoli.

The pioneers of submarine warfare in 1914-18 were the inspiration to the generation which followed in 1939-45, fighting in vastly superior submarines, but under the massive restrictions imposed by air power. The exclusive fraternity of holders of the Victoria Cross seem an élite apart—and so they deservedly are; yet those about whom this book is chiefly written were not unique, but a vivid cross-section of the very best of their contemporaries.

To win the supreme award when not in command was rarely possible, for life aboard a submarine throws the whole onus of decision on one man, in all but rare eventualities. The courage and initiative of the few exceptions is a measure of the calibre of the crews upon whom commanding officers relied with so much confidence. The extreme vulnerability of the submarine weds personnel to material in a sense not elsewhere achieved and demands team-work of the highest order.

It may surprise the general reader that in 1939-45 with instant communications allowing centralised control, individual submarines had such wide scope for independent action. But even the routine task was so precarious that only the man on the spot could know what was possible. Signals from headquarters needed to be informative rather than directive.

This book with its factual narrative shows how frequently opportunity offered. To seize it decisively required the exercise of superb courage, coolness and skill, called upon after months or even years of unflinching determination and endurance. Training and self-control must have developed an attitude of mind that allowed no compromise with the dedicated aim. War service in submarines produced other men with this invaluable mould of character who did not receive the Victoria Cross.

Off duty and on duty the essential man is the same. Linton, the rugby forward; Wanklyn, taking a trout on a dry-fly from a Dartmoor stream; Miers, playing any game with a gusto which swamped opposition—in war the thumb-nail sketch becomes the epic picture.

David Wanklyn as my First Lieutenant in peace and ace commanding officer in war was a close friend. The citation for his award quotes *Upholder's* action in sinking the heavily escorted troopship *Conte Rosso*. It is not the incident he would have selected. "Too large, like hooking a cannibal trout on a worm." Nor did the sinking of *Netunia* and *Oceania* quite suit. "A fluke, my gyro compass was out of action, I had to fire by eye." No, he would have chosen the sinking of the submarine *Ammiraglio St. Bon* at night with the only torpedo he had left, or perhaps his impudent destruction of the submarine *Tricheco* entering Brindisi harbour. Both examples of expert precision.

Sir William Jameson's accurate narrative and style devoid of superlatives provide the proper medium for recording these stirring deeds. He does not confine himself to the great events or forget the tedium of patrol and the strain of constant danger. In both World Wars it was a long, tough struggle which in my experience the minority survived.

I deeply appreciate the honour of subscribing a foreword.

G. W. G. SIMPSON
Whangaruru
New Zealand.

6th June 1962.

CHAPTER ONE

HOLBROOK AND B 11

ON Sunday 13 December 1914 the American vice-consul in Chanak went out in his row-boat for a little air and exercise. It was a beautiful morning, calm and clear. After skirting the Asiatic shore Mr C. Van H. Engert crossed to the Gallipoli side near Abydos, following much the same course as that so often pursued by Leander, swimming back from his nightly visits to the beautiful Hero. Engert was an expert oarsman and the current sluicing through the Hellespont, or Narrows, held no terrors for him. In the slacker water above Kilid Bahr he lay on his oars, looking about him and enjoying the winter sunshine. Suddenly the silence was shattered by a terrific explosion.

Some weeks earlier the Turkish battleship *Messoudieh* had been moored below Chanak in Sara Siglar Bay. Her broadside of two 9.2 inch and six 6 inch guns pointed past Kephez Point towards the open sea, protecting the Kephez minefield which, with the many forts on both shores, constituted one of the principal defences of the Dardanelles against the blockading Anglo-French fleet. Now the *Messoudieh* was enveloped in an enormous cloud of smoke through which the battleship was at first completely invisible. 'An internal explosion,' thought Mr Engert, but as he watched he heard the sound of heavy gunfire. Flashes of flame darted from the *Messoudieh*'s port battery and spouts of white water, rising from the calm blue sea between the battleship and Kephez Point, showed that she was aiming at a target quite close at hand, a target—invisible to Mr. Engert—which could only be an Allied submarine.

As suddenly as it had begun the firing ceased. The battleship began to list to port. Slowly at first, then more quickly she heeled over. The guns of the port battery disappeared under water, the funnels and masts tilted over the sea, and suddenly the great ship turned almost completely upside down until there was nothing to be seen except the curving whale-back of her bottom, swarming with little human figures. 'The whole affair,' wrote Mr. Engert a few lays later, 'had taken less than seven minutes.'

As he had been watching this extraordinary scene the current had carried Mr. Engert's boat much nearer and he now began to row towards the wreck. The *Messoudieh* had been lying in fairly shallow water and a good part of her hull remained above the surface. Joining in the work of rescue he helped to pick up men from the water and to release those imprisoned inside the upturned hull. Much later he had time to reflect on what he had seen, the first sinking of a battleship by a submarine, carried out in broad daylight fifteen miles inside heavily defended waters; an attack, to quote again from Mr Engert's report, 'so brilliant and daring that even Vice-Admiral Merten, the German officer in command at Dardanelles, admitted to me in conversation that 'it was a mighty clever piece of work' '.

The first Allied submarines had arrived off the entrance to the Dardanelles in August 1914. Turkey was still neutral, but the German battlecruiser *Goeben* and cruiser *Breslau,* escaping from the British Mediterranean fleet, had taken refuge in the Sea of Marmara. Both ships were now flying the Turkish ensign, on the pretext that they had been bought by the Ottoman Navy, but their German crews were known to be still aboard. Entry to the Dardanelles was prohibited to all foreign warships by Treaty, but a British and French fleet had assembled off Gallipoli. In November 1914 Turkey threw in her lot with the Central Powers and the blockading force had the additional duty of closing the Straits to all shipping.

Based on Tenedos was a mixed flotilla of British and French submarines, B 9, 10 and 11, the *Faraday*, *Le Verrier*, *Coulomb* and *Circé*, with the converted merchant ship *Hindu Kush* as a depot ship. All seven boats were elderly craft, dating from the early days of what was, in 1914, a new and unproved type of warship, for submarines had only been a really practical proposition since 1901.

The British 'B' class, built in 1907, were of primitive design, poor sea-boats on the surface and not very easy to handle submerged. 143 feet long, with a surface displacement of 285 tons, they were about one third the size of a modern "small" submarine. A single petrol engine gave a maximum surface speed of 12 knots and an electric motor, fed from storage batteries, could produce 6½ knots submerged, but only for one hour. To dive for longer periods speed must be very greatly reduced. These submarines had been designed for coastal defence, and the long journey of over 2000 miles to Malta, made before the war, and the further 1000 miles or so which had brought them to the mouth of the Straits had been something of a feat. Their machinery was unreliable and difficult to maintain in the very cramped space below. At sea the crew of two officers and eleven ratings worked, ate and slept amongst a complicated mass of pipes, valves, pumps, motors and other gear. Petrol as a fuel was a constant hazard, not only because of the danger of fire and explosion. Sometimes the fumes caused a form of drunkenness, with the same symptoms and an even more pronounced hangover. It was a little like living inside the bonnet of a motor car.

From early in December 1914 the Allied submarine flotilla kept up a dawn to dusk patrol off the entrance to the Dardanelles, and the view looking up the Straits was monotonously familiar. To the left the bare, brown hills of the Gallipoli peninsula plunged abruptly into the deep water skirting the European shore in a series of cliffs and ravines, with some flatter ground at Cape Helles on which was the fort at Sedd il Bahr, bombarded by the battleships of the Allied Fleet a few days after Turkey had entered the war. There were other guns and batteries further up the coast, but they were well concealed.

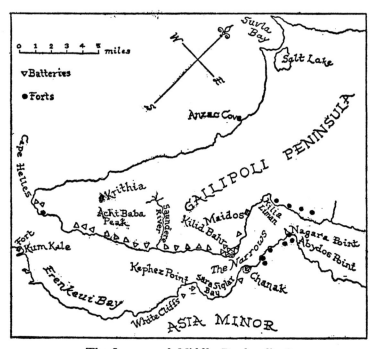

The Lower and Middle Dardanelles.*

The Asiatic shore on the right, also known to be well defended, was quite different; low, with sandy beaches skirting shallow bays, behind which a plain a mile or so in width was backed by gentle slopes. Wooded, cultivated, and dotted with small villages surrounded by orchards, it looked a green and pleasant land. About twelve miles from the submarines' patrol position the Straits seemed to end, where they bent northwards out of sight. Here, but invisible from the low elevation of a submarine's bridge, was Chanak and the entrance to the Narrows.

* The anti-submarine net stretched from Nagara Point to the Gallipoli bank. Gallipoli itself is twenty miles to the east.

Geography plays an important part in the events described in the next few chapters. The lower Dardanelles
is shaped like a Christmas stocking packed with mis-
cellaneous articles, the "foot" pointing nearly due north
between Chanak and Nagara, the "ankle" at the Narrows,
and the leg, running roughly N.E. – S.W., starting at
Kephez Point, bulging southward into the long stretch of
Eren Keui Bay and ending at the mouth of the Straits
between the points of Kum Kale on the Asiatic side and
Cape Helles on the tip of the Gallipoli Peninsula. Kum
Kale to Nagara is about fifteen miles. The width of the
Straits varies considerably; two miles at Kum Kale, over
four miles half way down the "leg", a mile and a half at
Kephez, three miles or so above the point in Sara Siglar
Bay, and a mere 1400 yards at the well-named Narrows
between Chanak and Kilid Bahr; wider again beyond this
point; narrow (a mile and a half) at Nagara. Beyond
Nagara are the Upper Straits, a wide stretch twenty miles
long extending to Gallipoli. It is thirty-five miles from
Kum Kale to the open waters of the Sea of Marmara.

For these old submarines, monotonously patrolling off
Kum Kale and Cape Helles, the Sea of Marmara was
indeed an unrealisable objective. If distance had been
the only obstacle they might have covered thirty-five miles
submerged, at a very slow speed. But the great rivers
emptying into the Black Sea, and the wind blowing from
the north east for nine months of the year, combine to
make the Bosphorus and Dardanelles more like rivers than
straits. The average strength of the current from
Gallipoli to the Mediterranean is one and a half knots.
with a maximum of no less than four knots in the
Narrows. From the Narrows to Kum Kale it runs at two
knots, and a 'B' class submarine, barely making headway
over the ground, could not expect to get much beyond
Chanak before its batteries were exhausted.

Nature put the Marmara out of reach, but there were
targets nearer home. The lower stretches of the Straits
around Eren Keui Bay were empty of shipping, but up

beyond Kephez there were constant signs of movement—the masts of small patrol craft coming and going and the superstructure of larger ships glimpsed above the sandy bulwark of the Point. The approaches to this area were well defended, with mines across the channel in the Kephez area and a great many guns covering the water. At night the beams of powerful searchlights swept the lower Straits.

Both British and French submarine crews were full of plans for something more adventurous than the dull routine of patrol. The French submarines, like the British, were old craft. They were, perhaps, even less suitable for a journey up the Straits than the 'B' boats, being steam driven. They had the additional disadvantage of being unable to dive deep, their small armament of torpedoes being in tubes outside the so-called pressure hull, the strong shell which is built to withstand the pressure when diving below the surface—15 lbs. per square inch for every thirty feet of immersion. Notwithstanding these disabilities the French crews were very keen and there was much rivalry between the two halves of the little flotilla. One of the Frenchmen had already penetrated above Sedd el Bahr. Lieutenant Holbrook in B 11 capped this by chasing a torpedo boat four miles beyond Kum Kale.

In December Lieutenant Commander Pownall, in command of the mixed flotilla, decided to send a submarine against the shipping at Chanak, and got approval to make the venture. B 11, the only British submarine with a new and reliable battery, was detailed for the job.

Put in its essentials the problem was this. The numerous guns along the shore covered the Straits at point-blank range. Day or night the trip would have to be made submerged, for the powerful searchlights sweeping the surface would easily pick out even such a small target as a submarine's conning tower in such confined waters. Submerged the submarine was invisible and safe from the guns, but it was known that there were at least five lines of mines moored across the Straits below Kephez

Point in addition to those in the Narrows. True, these mines had been laid against surface ships, and a submarine could dive below them.

Experience gained in the North Sea had shown that a submerged submarine could pass through such a minefield, by pushing the mooring wires aside, if steps were taken to prevent their being caught on any projection. Newer types of submarines had sloping guards around the hydroplanes (the horizontal diving rudders fitted near the bow and stern) and a 'jumping wire' running from stem to stern over the highest point on the conning tower, the top of the supports housing the periscope. Unfortunately the 'B' class had neither guards nor jumping wire. The nearest dockyard was at Malta nearly a thousand miles away, but the engineers of the depot ship, using what material was to hand, improvised the necessary guards and wires. Fitting the guards was another problem, but by flooding some of her ballast tanks B 11 managed to bring her hydroplanes far enough above the surface for the work to proceed. In the second week in December the job was done. Holbrook tested them against a simulated mine mooring—a wire, to which a heavy sinker was secured, suspended over the *Blenheim's* side on her main derrick. B 11, approaching from astern, steered directly for the wire. To everyone's satisfaction it was diverted by the guards, sliding harmlessly away astern. All was ready.

Norman Douglas Holbrook was twenty-six years of age. He had joined the Navy as a cadet thirteen years before. After serving in various surface ships he had volunteered for submarines and had been in them now for several years. Capable, thorough and self-confident, he did well in 'The Trade'. In August 1914 he was at Malta in B 11. It seemed a long way from the war, and his command, as even he regretfully admitted, was of little military value. But now his chance had come.

At 3.0 a.m. on 13 December B 11 cast off from the *Hindu Kush*. Wires splashed into the still water. The engine rumbled into life. Very soon the little submarine had disappeared into the darkness. At 4.15 a.m. Holbrook estimated that he was about three miles from Cape Helles, behind which the black lump of Gallipoli was distinguishable. To the eastward the mouth of the Straits was defined by the long beams of the searchlights, constantly sweeping the waters below the Kephez Point. Holbrook stopped his engine and settled down to wait. It had been noted that the searchlights were extinguished before dawn, when it was still dark. The sea was calm and the night very still. Little waves lapped gently against the sloping sides of the submarine. Behind him the open hatch gleamed faintly brighter from the blued lamps in the conning tower below.

At 5.0 a.m. the searchlights went out one by one. Starting her engine B 11, trimmed down so that little more than her small conning tower was above water, crept closer inshore. Twenty minutes later the dark shoreline, backed by the loom of the high ground running up to Achi Baba, was only a mile away. To starboard the sky over Asia Minor was lighter, but dawn was still some time off. Holbrook thought that there was just enough light to see through his periscope. He had already sent the lookout below and now he followed him down the hatch, pulling it shut and fastening the clips. There was something very final about this familiar action.

Remaining in the conning tower, where the single periscope of B 11 was situated, he called down to Winn, the First Lieutenant in the control room below. 'Flood main ballast. Twenty-five feet. Group up. Half ahead.' The order was repeated. Holbrook watched the greyness outside the glass scuttles of the conning tower change to inky black as B 11 slid under water. A minute later the submarine had levelled off at twenty-five feet.

Through the periscope he could still just distinguish the shore. It should be possible to navigate submerged, but there was a strange vibration, periodically passing through the hull and shaking the periscope. Holbrook climbed down into the control room, brightly lit after the gloom of the conning tower. He stood for a moment feeling the throbbing running through the deck under his feet. In the cramped interior the men stood and sat at their diving stations. The needles of the diving gauges were steady at twenty-five feet, but the vibration continued. He ordered 'slow' on the main motor; the vibration though reduced was still apparent. Something was wrong.

With daylight approaching he would have to act quickly. There was nothing aboard inside the boat to account for the vibration. Instantly Holbrook made up his mind. 'Surface. Blow main ballast.' Compressed air hissed through opened valves as it rushed into the tanks, expelling the water. Holbrook, back in the conning tower, watched the blackness give way to grey outside the glass scuttles, waited a moment and thrust open the conning tower hatch. A few drops of water splashed on him as he clambered out on to the wet and slippery deck. He looked aft over the whale-back, rising out of the sea, but there was nothing unusual to be seen. As B 11 gained full buoyancy Holbrook turned forward. Something was showing above the surface near the submarine's port bow. Part of the improvised guard around the port forward hydroplane had come away and the rest of the guard, bent out of shape, was standing up like a great claw.

Again Holbrook quickly made up his mind. It was impossible to go on like this, but he had no intention of turning back. The guard must be jettisoned, partly exposing the hydroplane, its shaft a hook to any mine mooring B 11 might encounter. But this was a risk which must be accepted. Calling down for his artificer to come on deck he ordered Winn to trim B 11 down by the stern, bringing the bow as high as possible.

It was lucky that the sea was so calm for it was an awkward job. Without a light two men, working half in and half out of the water, prevented from drifting away from the submarine by ropes secured under their arms, struggled with the bent and worse than useless guard. They worked quickly, loosening the bolts which secured it to the hull, though the delay seemed endless to Holbrook. He stood on the bridge bottling his impatience; watching the sky become lighter, the sea change from black to dark grey and the nearby shore defining itself. At any moment the flash of a gun might show that he had been spotted. But nothing untoward happened. By six a.m. B 11 was once more at periscope depth, rounding the point by Seddul Bahr and setting a course up the Straits.

Holbrook had carefully planned what he intended to do. He was a fisherman, and the narrow Straits, swept by the current, were not unlike a great river. He felt he had a pretty good idea as to how the all-important current, flowing at more than half the speed of little B 11, would behave. He would hug the European shore, steep-to and almost straight. The current would be strong here, but the water was deep and would flow past the cliffs without much turbulence. By keeping close to the peninsula he would avoid the whorls and eddies caused by the irregularities of the Asiatic shore with its shelving bottom and treacherous banks. But he had to avoid taking too much out of B 11's battery. At the maximum speed he dared to go, about 4 knots, he was only making good about 2 knots over the ground. The cliffs, only about a quarter of a mile away to port, passed by with maddening slowness as daylight grew.

He had planned to do this first leg of the journey— seven miles to the beginning of the Kephez minefield— at fifty feet, safely below any chance shipping he might encounter; but a new and totally unexpected trouble made this difficult. The water outside the Straits and in the upper layer inside was nearly fresh, but at fifty feet B 11 ran into a layer of much salter water which continually upset her trim. The submarine, her trim correct for fresh water, would become 'light' as soon as she struck the salt, and start to rise to the surface in spite of the efforts of the men on the hydroplanes to keep her down. Water would be admitted to the auxiliary tanks to correct this tendency, but it was necessary to come up to periscope depth at intervals to fix B 11's position. As she rose the submarine became 'heavy' and water had to be pumped out again. Nevertheless the journey continued, though with considerable effort. The hydroplanes were hand-worked in the primitive 'B' class, and stiff to move. Luckily he had on board an extra man, the coxswain of the spare submarine crew from the depot ship, who was able to relieve his own coxswain on the vital after hydroplanes.

For two and a half hours B 11 continued up the Straits, rising to periscope depth every forty-five minutes to fix her position. There is something about the atmosphere of a submarine, flavoured with the fumes of oil and battery gas, which gives men an excellent appetite, and breakfast was eaten in relays as they plunged along—cold tea, cold ham, bread, butter and jam. Holbrook himself consumed half a cold lobster, a last-minute present from one of the French submarine officers. There was little talk in the quiet, machinery-encumbered interior. Only essential lights were burning, to save the precious battery. Every member of the small crew knew his job, and did it without fuss or feathers. After two hours a man went round, checking the specific gravity of the cells. The battery was holding up quite well, but about a quarter of its capacity had been exhausted.

At 8.30 a.m. Holbrook picked out the mouth of the Suandere River on his port hand. B 11 was approaching the first of the five lines of mines across the Straits which made up the Kephez minefield. Ten minutes later, after a careful fix and a check of his course, Holbrook came down into the control room and ordered 'Eighty feet'. B 11 tilted a little, swam slowly to the new depth and levelled off. For the next hour they would be entirely 'blind', with nothing to guide them, very conscious of the lines of mines overhead and of the exposed hydroplane, ready to catch a mooring which passed too close and to drag down a mine on top of them. True, the horns of the mine were on its upper surface, but it was not a pleasant thought.

The hands of the clock crawled round as B 11 continued on her course. The inside of a dived submarine is very quiet. The hull acts as a sounding board and noises outside are easily heard. Ears were stretched for the sound of a wire scraping on the hull, but the next hour was uneventful, though a very long one. There was no patent log to give the exact distance covered, but at 9.30 a.m. Holbrook calculated, using the revolutions of the propellor shaft as his only guide, that they must be drawing clear of the minefield. At 9.40 he came to periscope depth for a look round. B 11 should be above Kephez Point, but without any real knowledge of the strength of the current below the surface there were many imponderables.

As B 11 rose slowly out of the depths Holbrook watched the water outside the conning tower ports change from dark to lighter blue. He put his eye to the periscope. Through the pale and shimmering water he could see the underside of the waves, a moving silver sheet. The top of the periscope broke through, dipped briefly under the bright water and stood clear.

Right ahead was a stretch of empty, sunlit water, but to port, and quite close, was the high ground of the peninsula. B 11 was a good deal further up the Straits than Holbrook had expected. Fine on the starboard bow and less than a mile away was a small town which must be Chanak, on the Asiatic shore at the entrance to the Narrows. To starboard, below the point on which it stood, low ground receded to make a deep bay. As Holbrook swung the periscope in this direction a large ship came into view on his quarter. Two big funnels on a high superstructure, a single mast; great guns fore and aft; a battleship.

Holbrook estimated that she was about a mile away, too far off for a certain hit with his little 18-inch torpedoes.

The strong current would take them off their course. Further, he was on the battleship's port bow, at an awkward angle. No one seemed to have seen B 11; indeed it was unlikely that the Turks were expecting an enemy so close at hand. Lowering the periscope Holbrook swung B 11 ninety degrees to starboard to close the range and to allow the current to sweep him down on to the battleship's beam. Five minutes later, with both torpedo tubes at the ready, he raised his periscope for another cautious look.

The battleship was much closer, almost filling the field of view of the periscope. He could see the Turkish ensign floating from her stern. There was still no sign of any unusual activity on board, though her guns, trained down the Straits, were now pointed directly at B 11. The current had been stronger than Holbrook had expected and was carrying B 11 rapidly across the mouth of the bay towards Kephez Point, but the battleship was still too far off for a certain hit. Holbrook went deep, corrected his course, and hung on for a few more breathless minutes. When he raised his periscope again the *Messoudieh* was less than half a mile away though the current, which must be very strong, had carried B 11 a little abaft her beam. Every detail of the big ship was now apparent; a sitting shot except for the accursed current. To allow for it Holbrook swung B 11 until she was pointing at the battleship's bow. FIRE!

He felt the submarine shudder and heard the cough of released compressed air as the torpedo left the starboard tube, and immediately ordered hard a-starboard, for the current was sweeping him dangerously inshore. B 11 dipped deeper as her bow swung to port, putting the top of the periscope under the surface, but Holbrook was able to see the track of his torpedo going straight towards the battleship before the water closed over the lens. He was still blind half a minute later when the submarine was violently shaken by the shock of an explosion. A hit!

A few seconds later the periscope broke surface again. Though stricken, the *Messoudieh* was still very much alive.

Immediately her guns began to fire. It was point-blank range and they made good shooting. Inside the submarine the crack of shells striking close overhead was clearly audible. Fountains of water springing up round the periscope sometimes hid the battleship, her guns stabbing flame, from view. Then B 11, slightly out of trim, dipped her periscope again. When Holbrook next saw the *Messoudieh* she was half-enveloped in a great cloud of smoke. She was settling by the stern and her guns had ceased firing.

But B 11 herself was now in difficulties. The current setting into the bay had carried her so far inshore that the sinking *Messoudieh,* which had been on B 11's starboard beam, was now on her port bow. It was essential to make at once for the open water in mid-channel. At this moment the man on the helm reported that the compass tube had flooded and that he could no longer see the card.

Holbrook had been concentrating on the attack and had only a rough idea of his position. He swung the periscope rapidly round to try and get a fix. Wherever he looked there was land. B 11 was deep inside Sara Siglar Bay, Kephez Point hiding the open water down the Straits, Chanak Point covering the Narrows, and the European and Asiatic shores completing the encirclement. The centre of the Straits must lie to the west, but being without a compass he could only make a guess as to where west might be. Pointing the submarine in what he judged to be the right direction he ordered the helmsman to steer as straight a course as possible. The compass card could not be seen but a dim shape was still visible in the frosted glass of the window at the end of the tube.

A torpedo boat had appeared and other vessels would no doubt be looking for him. He must get deep, below their rams. Ordering 'Fifty feet', Holbrook anxiously watched the depth gauge needle swinging down. But it had only reached thirty-eight feet when a shock shook the submarine, accompanied by the sound of sand scraping past the hull. B 11 was aground.

The five-fathom line in Sara Siglar Bay, close to which B 11 must have struck, follows a very irregular course. The direction in which deep water lay depended upon where she was, a fact about which Holbrook had very little exact information. He had to decide what to do, and do it very quickly. If he guessed wrong he would rapidly make matters worse. A dived submarine is virtually in a 'weightless' condition, very easily forced to the surface up a shelving bottom, by her own way or the force of the current. With her conning tower out of water B 11 would soon fall a victim to the guns of the forts on Chanak and Kephez Points.

'I put the helm hard-a-port,' wrote Holbrook in his report, 'and went on to full speed, the submarine frequently touching bottom from 10.10 to 10.20, when we got into deeper water.'

How simple it sounds! But for B 11's crew those ten minutes were a small lifetime. With the compass almost invisible Holbrook could not even be sure of holding a straight course. Sometimes B 11 would swim clear. A few seconds later there would be a grinding scrape as she once again grounded. With a torpedo boat close at hand he must keep deep, bumping along the bottom and anxiously watching the depth gauge. The compass was now completely fogged up and it was essential to come up for a fix. At 10.20 Holbrook cautiously brought B 11 to periscope depth. The sea around was clear and the *Messoudieh* had disappeared. Pointing B 11's bow directly at the European shore Holbrook, conning by verbal orders, held on. A few minutes later he could at last see open water to port. In mid-channel he turned B 11 down the Straits.

The long burst at full speed had taken a lot out of the battery; the lights were dim and safety was still sixteen miles away. He would have to husband his remaining resources carefully. B 11 proceeded at slow speed, her battery 'Grouped down', only making about $1\frac{1}{2}$ knots through the water, though now the current was behind

her. There was no question of diving under the Kephez
minefield, for without a compass the only way of keeping
on course was by raising the periscope at frequent intervals
to check direction.

The next hour was in many ways the most trying part
of the trip. Five lines of mines must be passed before they
regained the comparative safety of the lower Straits.
Eight hours of constant tension, rising to the climax of
the attack, were beginning to take their toll. It was over
five hours since the little submarine had dived off Cape
Helles, and the air was getting foul, slowing down
reactions at a time when it was essential to think clearly.
The minutes dragged slowly by as B 11, again hugging the
European shore, conned her way slowly along the Straits.

Luck was with them and by noon they had passed safely
through the minefield, dodging death by no one knew how
many inches. They were still right under the guns of the
forts on either hand and within easy reach of the patrols
no doubt searching for them. It would be suicide to come
to the surface for another nine or ten miles, but it was
possible to relax a little. Dinner was eaten in relays,
Holbrook finished his lobster and a tot of rum was issued
which made everyone feel much better. Sleep was what
they wanted now. The lights were dim; the battery
almost exhausted. Men and machine were running down.

Two hours later Holbrook estimated that B 11 was two
miles west of Cape Helles. There was a destroyer not far
away, but she was British. At last they could come to the
surface. After over eight hours submerged—a very long
time for such a small and primitive submarine—it was
good to see the light of the sun through the open conning
tower hatch and to climb out into the fresh air. How blue
the sea; how fine and free the sky! So foul was the air
inside the boat that the petrol engines refused to fire until
it had been turned for some time by the electric motor to
ventilate the engine room. Eventually it spluttered into
life, and B 11 set a course for Tenedos.

CHAPTER TWO

THE NARROWS

B 11 had proved that the difficulties of navigating the Straits submerged had not been exaggerated. Clearly B 9 and 10 with their worn-out batteries and the three small French submarines, unable to dive deep, could not be sent above the Kephez minefield. On the other hand Holbrook's exploit had demonstrated that a more modern boat, with much greater submerged endurance than B 11, might be able to get through the Narrows and reach the Sea of Marmara. No such submarine was immediately available but an 'E' boat of the Royal Australian Navy, AE 2, would shortly pass through the Suez canal into the Mediterranean. In the meantime, in response to Admiral Guépratte's requests, a French submarine of the 'jewel' class, arrived at Tenedos from Bizerta early in January.

The 'Saphir', which had been fitted with mine-guards in Malta Dockyard, had a stronger pressure hull, internal torpedo tubes and a high-capacity battery. For months her young commanding officer, Lieutenant de Vaisseau Henri de Fournier, had anticipated this moment, dreaming of diving into the Golden Horn at Constantinople where the battle-cruiser *Goeben* and modern cruiser *Breslau* were reported to be lying. At Malta, de Fournier had shown his plan for forcing the Straits to the staff of the British Commander-in-Chief, and impressed them by its thoroughness. As soon as the *Saphir* arrived off Gallipoli he reported on board the French flagship *Suffren*.

De Fournier was a man after Admiral Guépratte's own ardent heart, longing for action, confident in himself, his crew and his submarine. De Fournier wished to put his plan into action immediately, but Guépratte, assuring him that his chance would come in a few days, ordered him first to study local conditions by taking part in the ordinary dawn to dusk patrol off the mouth of the Straits. A great deal had been learnt by the British and French officers of the submarine flotilla—essential information for a successful attempt. On 15 January the *Saphir* sailed from Tenedos in the small hours for her first patrol, with orders to dive off Kum Kale and return to Tenedos that night. But de Fournier could not wait. He immediately turned north-east, up the Straits.

An hour later, at 7.20 a.m. the *Saphir*, swept by the set of the current into Eren Keui Bay, ran aground. The bottom was of sand and only gently sloping and de Fournier soon got off and continued his journey. Judging that he was approaching the Kephez minefield, he went to 70 feet. Twice, between 8.0 and 9.0 a.m., the crew heard mines bump on the outside of the casing. Several times mine mooring cables scraped along *Saphir's* side, the sounds of their passage clearly heard in the silent interior of the submarine. She passed safely under the minefield, but the pressure of the deep dive had started a leak in the hull behind some heavy electric cables near the starboard main motor. The leak was inaccessible, and the pumps, trying to keep down the level of the water rising in the bilges, were not functioning well. Nevertheless de Fournier decided to carry on. 'We will put things right this evening in the Marmara' he announced confidently.

At 11.30 a.m. the *Saphir* rose cautiously to periscope depth. De Fournier, fixing his position from marks on shore, decided he was in Sari Siglar Bay, between Kephez Point and Chanak. He was approaching the most difficult part of the passage, the Narrows. He went deep again, intending to remain at 70 feet for thirty-five minutes until he was above Chanak. Water was pouring from the leak, and steadily rising in the bilges, but for half an hour all went well. De Fournier watched the clock. In five minutes *Saphir* was due to come up for another look round.

Suddenly there was a shock followed by continuous scraping.

The submarine, forced off her course by the tide, had struck the Asiatic shore near Chanak, where the water shoals rapidly. In a few seconds the bow had run up this underwater slope and broken surface. *Saphir*, at a steep angle to the horizontal, was in desperate straits. Her speed and the current had driven her hard aground. Going full astern on both motors failed to move her so the Captain ordered the forward main ballast tanks to be blown. *Saphir* commenced to move, rapidly gathering stern-way, but appallingly out of trim. Before the ballast tanks could be flooded again she was at an angle of more than 45 degrees by the stern. Acid spilled out of her batteries and ran into the bilges, already half-full of seawater. Pungent chlorine gas made the crew gasp and choke as they struggled to get *Saphir* under control.

At a depth of over 220 feet *Saphir* hit the bottom and at last levelled off. The pressure, more than 100 lbs. per square inch, was distorting the hull, starting other leaks from which water cascaded into the boat. Even in the control room it was ankle deep. In a very short time the electrical machinery would be put out of action. De Fournier must act quickly.

Ordering the main ballast to be blown he tried to force *Saphir* to the surface, but the depth gauges showed no movement. As a last resort he ordered the two emergency drop keels, each of about ten tons, to be released. Relieved of their weight the submarine at last left the bottom. Now she rose quickly. Breaking surface, she was greeted by heavy fire from field guns and a fort. By flooding all main ballast *Saphir* got under before she was hit, but the boat was uncontrollable, taking on big angles. There was nothing for it but to come up again. De Fournier climbed on to the bridge, conned his submarine into mid channel and gave the order for the crew to abandon ship. The last up was his second in command, who had flooded the ballast tanks as he left the control room. The *Saphir* plunged out of sight, leaving her crew in the ice-cold water. Some managed to swim ashore, but de Fournier, his second in command and twelve of the twenty-five ratings were swept away by the current.

None of this was known at the time. No news of the *Saphir* reached the flotilla outside the Straits. She had simply disappeared. With her loss there was again no submarine available with sufficient endurance to attempt the passage of the Dardanelles; but in February, AE 2 arrived at Tenedos.

The British 'E' class, which had been coming into service just before the war, had already proved themselves in the North Sea and Baltic. Displacing 652 tons on the surface and 795 tons submerged they were not only considerably larger than the 'B's, but a great improvement technically. The ballast tanks instead of being internal, spoiling the circular shape of the pressure hull and weakening it considerably, were in the form of 'saddle' tanks outside. Diesel engines, using oil instead of the dangerous and toxic petrol as fuel, gave the useful surface speed of 15 knots. A large battery gave a theoretical endurance of about fifty miles submerged, though only at $2\text{-}2\frac{1}{2}$ knots. The torpedo armament was more than double that of a 'B'—two bow tubes, two beam tubes and a single tube in the stern, firing 18-inch torpedoes. Larger periscopes, passing right down into the control room, permitted the conning tower to be shut off when diving.

Lieutenant Commander H. G. Stoker of AE 2 immediately began to study the problem of forcing the Straits, and in particular the passage of the Narrows. Even for surface ships the Narrows were a navigational hazard, with sharp turns at Chanak and Nagara and strong 'sets' into the bays on either shore. At the narrowest point, where the channel was only 1400 yards wide, the current flowed at no less than 4 knots. Nowhere was it less than $2\frac{1}{2}$ knots and something like full speed would have to be used for about four miles—a heavy drain on the battery

Intelligence believed (accurately, as it proved) that

there were five lines of mines between Sara Siglar Bay
and Nagara, but in such constricted waters it would
clearly be impossible to run deep for long periods. Most
of the passage would have to be made at periscope depth.
All the waters through which he would have to pass were
heavily patrolled by surface craft and the Turks had
mounted guns along both shores, covering the Narrows
and its approaches at point-blank range. The high speed
necessary to make way against the current meant that the
periscope would leave a considerable wake, and it was
highly unlikely that a submarine would escape detection.
Nor was this all. He would have to remain submerged
until he had passed Gallipoli—a dive of about 35 miles,
against an *average* current of 1½ knots. A simple calcula-
tion made it evident that the capacity of even an 'E' boat's
battery was only just sufficient for the journey. Nevertheless Stoker thought it could be done.

His arrival off Gallipoli had coincided with the start
of the Allied attempt to force the passage of the Straits
with surface ships, a plan which aimed at destroying the
forts by gunfire. Bombardment of the outer forts began in
late February. Progress was slow, but in early March ships
could penetrate as far as Eren Keui Bay.

With his plan in his pocket Stoker set out for Mudros
on 7 March to lay his scheme before the Commander-in-
Chief, Admiral Carden. But his luck was out. Because
of an alteration, of which Stoker was unaware, in the
position of a leading mark, AE 2 ran ashore near the
entrance to the harbour, suffering damage which could
only be repaired in a dockyard. Bitterly disappointed,
Stoker sailed for Malta.

On 18 March the British and French Fleets made their
great effort to reduce the forts in the Kephez area as a
preliminary to sweeping up the mines and forcing the
Narrows. Sixteen heavy ships entered the mouth of the
Straits and opened a terrific bombardment. At first the
operation went well, but an unsuspected minefield
recently laid by the enemy in Eren Keui Bay did great

execution. Three battleships were sunk, a battle cruiser damaged and the fleet withdrew without accomplishing its objective. It was now decided to mount a combined naval and military attack. Whilst troops and equipment were being assembled the Turks strengthened the defences from Kephez to Nagara, laying additional mine-fields and bringing up more guns.

On 27 March three of the crack E boats from England, E 11, E 14 and E 15, sailed from Portsmouth to reinforce the Dardanelles Flotilla. Touching at Gibraltar to complete with fuel they reached Malta on 7 April. The reliability of the machinery of submarines left a good deal to be desired in those days, and E 11 had developed a serious fault in a shaft for which no spare was available. Leaving her in the Dockyard E 14 and E 15 sailed again next day, reached Mudros on 9 April and secured along-side the submarine depot ship *Adamant* which had accompanied them from England. E 14's diesel engines were giving trouble, but after three days and nights of continuous work both submarines were ready for action on 12 April.

The Turkish forces in Gallipoli were almost entirely dependent on seaborne traffic through the Marmara for their supplies; the nearest railway was several days' march away along rough and narrow roads. A submarine in the Marmara could attack the enemy at a vital point. With the date for Allied landings on the peninsula drawing nearer it had become imperative to interfere with Turkish communications; but could a submarine get through the Straits whose defences had so recently hurled back the Fleet? When on 12 April the Commanding officers of E 14 and E 15 were summoned to a conference on board the flagship *Queen Elizabeth,* few in that Fleet expected much in the way of results.

The Chief-of-Staff, Commodore Roger Keyes, was in the chair. Fortunately Keyes, though not himself a sub-mariner, had been Commodore (Submarines) before the war, and had commanded the overseas submarine flotilla based on Harwich until appointed to the Mediterranean. At a time when enthusiasm for the new weapon amongst many naval officers outside the submarine service was distinctly lukewarm he was a great believer in the possibilities of the submarine. Four years of close association with the young submarine commanding officers had made him their ardent admirer.

The problem could be simply stated. Could a submarine penetrate the Straits, and remain long enough in the Sea of Marmara, entirely unsupported, to inflict worthwhile damage on the enemy?

From the first the *military* defences of the Straits were regarded as a surmountable hazard by all the submarine officers present. Mines had fully demonstrated their deadliness on 18 March, but minefields could, with luck, be negotiated. A submerged submarine was almost safe from gunfire; the depth charge had not been invented and the numerous patrols had only the ram as a weapon, which a submarine could escape by going deep. As Stoker had earlier decided it was in navigating the Narrows and remaining submerged long enough to reach Gallipoli that the greatest danger lay. The submarines would have to con their way through narrow and unfamiliar waters swept by strong currents without any modern navigational aids such as radar or echo-sounding, fixing their position by what they could see through a periscope whose window was only a few feet about the surface and was probably under heavy fire. Patrols attempting to ram might force the submarine to go deep at critical moments. Any error here might easily bring a submarine to the surface where it would quickly fall a victim to gunfire at close range. Torpedo tubes were also known to have been fixed on shore at certain points.

Even if the Narrows could be negotiated the problem of reaching the Marmara was a matter of mathematics and conjecture. Could the initial dive be postponed long enough and the submerged speed kept low enough to allow a submarine to gain open water, where she could risk coming to the surface, before the battery was completely exhausted? Because of the current a comparatively high average speed was essential and something approaching full power would have to be used when passing through the Narrows.

The only accurate data available was of the strength of the *surface* currents. It was hoped that the current was weaker thirty or more feet below the surface, and the Black Sea Pilot contained brief and unsupported references to a deep counter-current running *up* the Straits under certain unspecified conditions of wind and tide and at an unknown depth.* A submarine might expect some help from these factors, but how much?

The problem was briefly set out by Lt. Comd. C. G. Brodie of Keyes's staff. With the mouth of the Straits in Allied hands it should be possible to remain on the surface for a few miles, until put down by the searchlights, thus shortening the submerged journey by six or seven miles. Passing under the Kephez minefield at moderate speed a submarine would have about three quarters of its battery power unused when it began the high-speed section, from below Chanak to above Nagara. Would there be enough left after this for the long final leg submerged to east of Gallipoli? Somerville, the Captain of the *Adamant,* Boyle of E 14 and Pownall, who had been on the spot for six months, were very doubtful. The last to be asked for his opinion was the commanding officer of E 15, T. S. Brodie, C. G. Brodie's twin brother.

'I think it could be done,' he said.

Keyes, always ready to take the more adventurous line, quickly made up his mind. The stakes justified the risk.

'Well, It's got to be tried, and you shall do it.'

Next day T. S. Brodie was flown over the Straits in an R.N.A.S. seaplane piloted by Lieutenant Commander

* Both the Bosphorus and Dardanelles have this counter-current on occasions. It was discovered, it is said, when a Sultan ordered that an unwanted wife should be flung into the Bosphorus. She reappeared, somewhat disconcertingly, opposite his palace next day.

Samson. The weather was fine and clear. From 4000 feet the blue ribbon of the Dardanelles, winding between the hilly peninsula of Gallipoli and the flatter, fertile Asiatic shore, looked uncommonly narrow. Off the points of Kephez, Chanak and Nagara the sandbanks lying close below the surface were clearly visible. In the Narrows streaks of darker water marked the edges of the swirling current. Turkish patrol craft hurried about. Stabs of flame and puffs of smoke showed where some of the many batteries were located. Though the enemy anti-aircraft fire was inaccurate, the guns could scarcely fail to hit a submarine which broke surface in the Straits below.

That night E 15, every available corner packed with provisions for a three-week patrol, was ready. At the last moment the drive of one of the hydroplanes became defective, but the engineers had the trouble rectified by midnight.

Brodie was quietly confident. At 2.30 a.m. he was lying off the *Queen Elizabeth* to embark a Lieutenant R.N.V.R. with local knowledge (he had been vice-consul at Chanak) who could act as an interpreter and help in identifying marks on shore. As E 15 sailed, the flagship signalled a message from the First Lord, Mr. Winston Churchill.

'I wish you God speed in your hazardous enterprise.' A few minutes later the submarine had disappeared into the darkness.

At the mouth of the Straits Brodie partly flooded his main ballast tanks, bringing E 15 lower in the water to reduce her silhouette. He proceeded slowly on the surface for some miles before deciding that the flashes of brilliance from the great searchlights sweeping the Straits were making him too conspicuous. Stopping his diesel engines he flooded all main ballast and dived to periscope depth. Shortly afterwards E 15 went deep to ninety feet to pass under the minefield.

B 11, hugging the European shore, had experienced considerable difficulty in holding a trim in the mixture of fresh and salt water, and Brodie aimed to keep nearer to the centre of the channel. This plan seemed to be successful and the long minutes passed without incident. When he judged that he was in Sari Siglar Bay above the minefield he gave the order to come to periscope depth. It would be daylight now and he could get a fix from landmarks on shore.

E 15 had been diving through a layer of fairly salt water and was 'heavy' when she rose into the lighter fresh water above. She spent several minutes 'catching a trim' in the new layer and was still running deep when a noise like a shower of hail on the hull indicated that she had struck bottom. Her own way and the force of the current carried her quickly up the slope of a sandbank. The current caught the bow and swung it to starboard so that E 15 was pointing well off course. In a matter of seconds her conning tower and casing were clear of the water, right under the guns of Fort Dardanos on the Asiatic shore just below Kephez Point.

The Turks were keeping a sharp lookout and instantly opened fire. One of the first shells penetrated the conning tower, killed poor Brodie and let in a flood of salt water which cascaded into the control room and very soon found its way into the battery below. Choking clouds of chlorine gas welled up, suffocating six of the crew. E 15, hard and fast aground, holed and unable to dive, was doomed.

C. G. Brodie, flying above the Straits later that morning, saw a cigar-shaped object in the shallows below Kephez Point. It was his brother's submarine. Smoke drifted from her. The attempt had failed.

It remained to make sure that E 15 was entirely destroyed, a little saga in itself in which B 11 was frustrated by fog and B 6 almost lost by running aground close to E 15. Two destroyers, blinded by searchlights, were driven off by gunfire. Finally picket boats carrying torpedoes succeeded, in an exploit of great gallantry, in hitting E 15, blowing a great hole in her side. Brodie had failed but his submarine would never serve the enemy.

The result of this attempt was not encouraging. Lieut.

Commander Boyle in E 14 was ready, fully provisioned and stored. On 21 April, Stoker in AE 2 returned from Malta. But the loss of E 15 had raised grave doubts about the practicability of forcing the Straits.

A great host of vessels was now assembled off Gallipoli. The landings on the peninsula were to take place on 25 April and the importance of getting at the Turkish lines of communication was greater than ever. Stoker, though his crews had scarcely had time to 'shake down' and regain full efficiency after their weeks in the dockyard, was burning with enthusiasm. Knowing that he had studied the passage of the Straits in great detail, Admiral de Robeck gave his consent for AE 2 to make her attempt. In the small hours of 23 April AE 2 closed the Straits, trimmed down until her conning tower was awash and advanced towards the probing searchlights, only to be frustrated at the last moment by the fracture of a shaft in her hydroplane gear as she dived off the Suandere River. There was nothing for it but to turn round and come back, but by nightfall the defective shaft had been replaced and AE 2 was again ready. It was 24 April, the eve of the landings, and Stoker was told he could try again. Besides attempting to reach the Marmara he was to attack any ships capable of laying mines sighted in Sari Siglar Bay or above Chanak.

Diving just before dawn, when he was fired at from near Suandere, Stoker stayed at twenty feet whilst the light increased, gradually revealing leading marks ashore. He got a good fix and went deep under the Kephez minefield. When he came to periscope depth again he was further up than he had anticipated, opposite Sara Siglar Bay below the Narrows. Stoker later described his experiences in the Narrows very vividly in his book 'Straws in the Wind'.* Rappings and scrapings on the hull indicated that he was passing right through the middle of the Chanak minefield. Twice something very much more

* "Straws in the Wind" by Commander H. G. Stoker D.S.O. Herbert Jenkins, 1925.

solid than a mooring bumped the hull. For several minutes a loose object, whose nature could readily be imagined, was caught up on some projection on the submarine, knocking against the hull at intervals until it broke clear.

He was forced to rise frequently to periscope depth to check his position. The sea was absolutely calm, and each time AE 2 showed her periscope heavy fire was opened from either shore. From inside the submarine shells could be heard cracking into the water, harmless enough as long as AE 2 kept her depth, but instantly lethal if an error in navigation forced her to the surface.

Near Chanak, Stoker sighted a ship which looked like a minelayer, fired a torpedo, and had the satisfaction of feeling a heavy shock as the shot went home. He was unable to watch his victim (it was a Turkish gunboat which he had sunk) as the gyro compass chose that moment to 'wander', putting AE 2 off course. In a moment she had been caught by the current, swept ashore, and driven half to the surface on Chanak Point, luckily so close under the guns of Fort Chemenlik that they could not be depressed sufficiently to hit her. With the compass still wandering AE 2 got back into deep water, only to run ashore again a few minutes later on the opposite side of the Straits, this time right under the Derma Burnu Battery on the European shore. Again she got off, negotiated the sharp turn off Nagara Point, and was at last able to see clear water ahead; the long leg to Gallipoli.

But her battery was very low, the enemy thoroughly aroused and Stoker thought he would try and shake off the patrols, which attacked his periscope each time he showed it above water and constantly rumbled overhead, by lying doggo until dark. Finding the bottom at 70 feet off Kangali he settled down to wait. Patrol craft, their propellor beats clearly heard in the silent submarine, continued to pass overhead until nightfall. Not until 8.45 p.m., when AE 2 had been submerged for sixteen hours, was there a lull. She surfaced, started her diesel engines, and began to charge and pump up her air bottles, which like the battery were nearly exhausted. In relays the crew had a few minutes on deck for a blessed draught of cool night air and a look at the stars which many of them must have wondered if they would ever see again. Two hours later Stoker was able triumphantly to signal to Admiral de Robeck his arrival in the Sea of Marmara. The news that an Australian submarine had accomplished the feat was immediately passed to the Australian troops who had landed that morning on the west side of Gallipoli, in the place ever afterwards known as Anzac Cove. So far AE 2 had been very fortunate. Would her good luck hold?

CHAPTER THREE

BOYLE AND E 14

AT 1.35 a.m. on 27 April E 14 weighed anchor, sailed from Tenedos and closed the Straits on the surface, passing between the numerous ships anchored off Cape Helles. From the peninsula flickers of flame and the rumble of gunfire showed that fighting was in progress on the beaches. A hospital ship, huge red crosses on her floodlit side, was embarking the wounded. Soon all this was left astern as E 14 followed the dark and silent European shore behind the Turkish lines towards Suandere.

At 3.45 a.m. she passed into the area swept by the searchlights; at White Cliffs on the starboard bow, above Suandere on the port. The great beams swung steadily over the water, briefly lighting up the men on the bridge, but it was several minutes before the enemy gave any sign of having sighted the submarine. Then the searchlight on the European shore paused in its sweep, resting steadily upon them. A few seconds later shells plunged into the water close ahead. As the captain, Lieutenant Commander E. C. Boyle, followed the others down the conning tower, closing the upper lid behind him, E 14 slid below the surface.

It was too dark to see anything through the periscope so Boyle went to 70 feet on the course he had already worked out. After a time he ordered 'Twenty feet', cautioning his First Lieutenant not to break surface. The periscope was still useless so he went deep again. Except for a gentle hum from the motors and the intermittent sound of the steering and hydroplane machinery it was very quiet in the submarine. E 14 had a well-trained crew.

Few orders were necessary. Each man knew exactly what he had to do, and did it.

When AE 2 reported her arrival in the Sea of Marmara, E 14 was immediately ordered to follow her. At the conference a fortnight earlier Boyle had expressed the opinion that the passage of the Straits was impracticable. That had been his view, but it had not prevented him from making very careful preparations for an attempt if called upon to do so. Except for topping up with fresh water and stores he was completely ready.

Edward Courtney Boyle, 33 years of age, was one of the most experienced submarine officers in the Navy. He had been given his first command, Holland 1, in 1903. Patrolling in the Heligoland Bight in D 3 after the outbreak of war he had been mentioned in Despatches. He had then taken over E 14, completing at the Barrow-in-Furness yard of Vickers Ltd.

Even as a cadet Boyle, quiet, poised and effective, had shown promise. Appointed a cadet captain he controlled his fellows without fuss and apparently without much effort. After a few years in surface ships he volunteered for service in submarines. At that time many of the officers in the new Branch were unconventional men, readily distinguishable by their cheerful disregard of the uniform regulations. Boyle remained his neat, somewhat enigmatic self, quietly 'ganging his own gait'. Had it not been for the excellent results he invariably produced he might have been dismissed as a looker-on at life, a little too aloof to be personally involved. Reserved, but courteous; unenthusiastic, but always somehow at the head of the hunt. In a branch of the Service where personalities counted for a great deal he had the absolute confidence of his crew. Forethought, excellent discipline and a complete grasp of his profession ensured that his submarines were rarely afflicted with the many troubles which often beset their fellows.

Called upon to face their greatest test Boyle and his

men were quietly confident. This is what Leading Stoker J. T. Haskins wrote in his diary on 26 April:

'Orders to get ready to go through the Dardanelles, plenty of excitement, soon be in the thick of it.'

The first leg of the long dive, under the Kephez mine-field to opposite Sara Siglar Bay, was without incident, but when Boyle rose to periscope depth to fix his position he found himself further above Kephez Point than he had expected. Evidently the current at seventy feet was weaker than anticipated. This was all to the good, but it would not help him much on the difficult leg through the Narrows, where he must come to periscope depth at very frequent intervals for navigational purposes.

Approaching Chanak, Boyle increased speed. E 14 was now moving through the water at 7 knots, but only making good about 3 knots over the land, because of the adverse current. The critical leg from Chanak to Nagara would take about an hour, but Boyle, determined to save his battery, kept to his planned speed. He now remained at periscope depth, believing that faulty navigation was a greater hazard than the minefields. Every few minutes he cautiously raised the periscope for a quick look round.

He was approaching Nagara, still undetected by the enemy, when he sighted a gunboat. It was a long shot for those days, about 1600 yards, and the target was at an awkward angle, nearly stern on, but Boyle decided to fire. The torpedo missed and the splash of its discharge gave him away, drawing a heavy fire from both banks. Inside the boat they could hear the sharp crack of shells hitting the water overhead. 'All the forts firing at me', said his brief official report later. The other bow tube was now fired. Boyle watched the track of his torpedo running true, and saw a column of smoke and water rise up by the gunboat.* Suddenly the periscope went completely dark.

What had happened? Had it been hit? Ordering the other periscope to be raised Boyle saw an extraordinary sight. A few feet away was a Turkish picket boat. From it

* He had, in fact, sunk the Turkish gunboat *Berki-Satvet*.

a man was leaning, clutching E 14's other periscope in his hands! A sporting effort, and if he had had a pal with a hammer serious damage might be done, so Boyle hurriedly went deep.

He had passed Chanak at 5.15 a.m. At 6.30 a.m. he successfully rounded Nagara Point. The Turks were thoroughly roused; many patrolling craft always seemed to be about and the periscope was frequently fired on, but it was now possible to stay deep for longer periods. Unfortunately when running blind he now passed quite close to the old battleship *Muin I Zaffer*, only sighting her when she was a long way out of range astern. Boyle, whose orders were to concentrate on supply ships for Gallipoli, did not turn back.

At 9.15 a.m., five and a quarter hours after diving, E 14 passed Gallipoli. She was in the Marmara, but still being harassed by the very active Turkish patrols, not very lethal so long as she kept under, but able to put her out of action very easily if she came to the surface. The battery was getting low. At 3.40 p.m. Boyle came up and started to charge, but was put down twenty minutes later. Every unnecessary light, the ovens and even the tea urns had been switched off to save current. E 14, her battery almost exhausted, could only proceed at very slow speed. She could not move away and it was nearly four hours before the patrols took themselves off. Just before 8.0 p.m. the specific gravity of the battery was down to 1140, a very low figure. Boyle again surfaced, started his diesel engines and began to pump back the vital current.

'We were all very happy,' wrote his young navigating officer Lieutenant R. W. Lawrence later, 'and everyone started congratulating everyone else—We had our first meal at 8.0 p.m., and after the excitement of the day, it was a hearty one.'

But only three quarters of an hour later they were put down again. Fortunately the light was now going and when Boyle surfaced after dark he was able to remain up long enough to make some impression on the battery, before being chased under by a destroyer just before 11.0 p.m.

It had been a busy day. Between 4.0 a.m. and 9.18 p.m. E 14 had been submerged for 16 hours 14 mins., including a dive of 11 hours 40 minutes, the longest she had ever done. The battery, whose specific gravity when fully charged was 1240, was still only 1160. They had broken through the Straits, but the work they had been sent out to do was just beginning.

At 1.0 a.m. next day Boyle again came to the surface and charged for an hour and a half before being put under. It was 6.30 a.m. before the sea was clear, and the battery was still low. It was a glorious morning, calm and still. Both shores of the Marmara, only fifteen miles wide at its western end, were in sight, with little villages set on the green slopes running down to the sparkling blue sea. The air was absolutely clear, an unfortunate feature of the Sea of Marmara from the submariner's point of view, for on nine days out of ten visibility is so good that a submarine on the surface can be spotted a long way off. It was not very long before a destroyer appeared, sending the crew, who had been smoking and sunning themselves on deck, hurrying below to their diving stations. It was only what Lawrence described as a 'very third rate destroyer', but E 14, helpless on the surface and with orders to reserve her precious torpedoes for supply ships, had to dive, and remain under until the destroyer had left the vicinity. This cat-and-mouse business continued all day, with E 14 spending short periods on the surface, only to be put down again. But from 7.30 p.m. Boyle was able to charge for four and a half hours before a destroyer, suddenly spotted against the dark loom of the land, put him under. The battery was now fairly well up so he remained submerged, running deep until 5.0 a.m. next day to give the crew a badly needed rest.

By breakfast time the battery was fully charged for the first time since E 14 entered the Marmara 36 hours before. So far no worthwhile supply ships had been seen, but early that afternoon they sighted two transports escorted by three destroyers. The sea was absolutely calm, without a breath of wind to ruffle the glass-like surface, but Boyle crept within 800 yards unobserved and fired at the leading transport. The torpedo missed or failed to explode, but its track gave E 14 away and the 'splash' of the discharge indicated her position to the destroyers, which opened fire and tried to ram. Boyle fired his other bow tube at transport number two before going deep to get out of the way. A destroyer rumbled harmlessly overhead, but a lucky shot had damaged the window of one periscope, starring the glass and making it virtually useless. E 14 was still 'deep' when she felt the shock of an explosion; the depth gauge needles jumped 10 feet. When she rose again to periscope depth one of the transports had turned towards the shore, low in the water and belching clouds of white and yellow smoke.

That evening E 14 sighted another submarine on the surface. It was AE 2 and for some time the two E-boats lay together exchanging news.

Boyle had been submerged for forty-five of the sixty-four hours since he had dived off Suandere. E 14's main motors were running rather hot after such continuous use, but apart from this she was in excellent shape. Stoker also had no defects, but he had fired nearly all his torpedoes and asked Boyle to let him have one or two. Boyle, with only six of his ten 'fish' remaining, and a long patrol ahead, was unable to comply. Stoker turned away north-west to complete charging his battery on the surface, after arranging a further rendezvous. Boyle turned west to get in touch with his Admiral outside the Straits by wireless. Because of the limited range of his set he could only do this from the western end of the Marmara.

The news that AE 2 and E 14 had entered the Marmara had raised the keenness of the French submarine crews to boiling point. The gallant and warm-hearted Admiral Guépratte was delighted at the British success, but even more anxious that the French submarines should participate in the glories of forcing the Straits. None of his submarines, small vessels of less than 400 tons, had the necessary submerged endurance for the long journey into the Marmara, but Admiral de Robeck agreed that they should try to go as far as the Narrows and attack shipping between Chanak and Nagara.

The French Admiralty had recently despatched the *Bernouilli* and the *Joule* to reinforce the flotilla. On 29 April Lieutenant de Vaisseau Defforges in the *Bernouilli* passed successfully under the Kephez minefield, but was still below the Narrows four hours after diving off Kum Kale. A torpedo, which missed, was fired at a Turkish destroyer. The *Bernouilli*, which had taken too much out of her battery on the way up and during the attack, now found herself in difficulties. Unable to make headway against the strong current she turned back and withdrew to Tenedos.

Two days later the *Joule* left Tenedos soon after midnight. Her captain, Lieutenant de Vaisseau Aubert du Petit-Thouards, descendant of a famous French family of seamen, was determined to do better than the *Bernouilli*. Entering the Straits in the darkness he was due to surface again outside before nightfall, but sunset came and there was no news of him. The battleship *Agamemnon*, on patrol off Kum Kale, now reported that she had picked up the air vessel of a torpedo of French manufacture floating down the Straits that afternoon. The numbers stamped on it identified it as belonging to the *Joule*. Next morning the Turkish wireless communiqué announced the destruction of a submarine in the minefield. *Joule* had been sunk with all hands. Three out of the six submarines which had attempted to pass the Narrows had now been lost, and there was a report from Constantinople that the Turkish torpedo boat *Sultan Hissar* had picked up survivors from the Australian AE 2 which she had destroyed by gunfire.

This report alas, was all too true. AE 2 and E 14 had cruised a few miles apart on the morning after their

46

meeting. When they separated AE 2, patrolling along the southern shore, sighted a Turkish torpedo boat. Stoker was attempting an attack with his one remaining torpedo when AE 2 struck a patch of salt water, lost her trim and broke surface within a mile of her quarry. The torpedo boat opened fire, approached at full speed, and almost succeeded in ramming Stoker before he got under. Trimmed very heavy AE 2 now ran out of the salt-water patch, which had brought her up, into lighter fresh water, took on a big angle by the bow and began to go down. The water was very deep and Stoker, fearing he might get below the depth his pressure hull could stand, reversed his motors. Before her crew had fully regained control AE 2 had again broken surface quite close to the torpedo boat, which quickly put several shells through the hull. Water gushed into the engine room as Stoker ordered all hands on deck, remaining with his First Lieutenant, Lieutenant Price, to open the valves flooding the tanks before following them up the hatch. AE 2 plunged to the bottom. Stoker and his crew were picked up and made prisoners, but they had blazed the trail.

The destruction of AE 2 and the *Joule* on successive days had brought the losses to four and underlined the hazards of the task confronting the Allied submarines. Against this sombre background the signals from E 14, which reached the British flagship nearly every night, were particularly welcome.

E 14, continuing her lone patrol, was not having an easy time. Because of the danger of being surprised on the surface in the darkness Boyle preferred to dive until dawn and charge his batteries in daylight, but the weather continued fine and clear and he was constantly put under by the very active Turkish patrols. The shipping line from Constantinople to Gallipoli follows the northern coast of the Marmara, and E 14 was rarely out of sight of land. The smoke of fires lit on shore would warn supply ships of her presence and bring the patrols hurrying up to put her down. Boyle was also greatly handicapped by having no gun, for the enemy were using many quite small craft for carrying supplies. On 30 April he sighted a tug towing four heavily laden dhows, chased on the surface and managed to make them stop by firing at the tug with a rifle. This took so much time that a gunboat appeared before the dhows could be boarded and sunk with demolition charges.

That night he reported to the Fleet by wireless, surfacing close inshore at the western end of the Marmara. It was flat calm, very dark and absolutely still. The crackle and flash of sparks dancing on the overcharged aerial seemed, to the men crowded on the conning tower, smoking and getting a draught of fresh air, to be sure to draw patrols to the vicinity. Instinctively they dropped their voices. Suddenly a great light flared up on the shore, only half a mile away. Boyle ordered the operator to stop transmitting and sent the men below. For a while nothing happened. Then Lawrence saw a moving shape and a bow wave which might be an enemy destroyer. E 14 slid under the surface. The bottom was conveniently close and free of rocks, so she rested there until dawn.

On 1 May Boyle decided he would teach the Turkish patrols, which must be now thinking they could approach with impunity, a lesson:

'Came up to 22 feet at 4.50 a.m.,' (wrote Leading Stoker Haskins in his diary) 'but nothing in sight. We ran along at 40 feet until 7.0 a.m., then we surfaced and proceeded on our way on the gas engine. Breakfast on salmon and biscuits and was ready for anything. At 10.12 a.m. we sighted enemy ships right under the land. We dived and closed in on an armed minelayer. At 600 yards range we fired one torpedo; it was running true. The Captain saw two men aboard the minelayer cleaning a gun aft; they saw the torpedo coming straight at them, and they started to run to tell the officer on the bridge. But they were too late. The torpedo hit her and she blew up; by the explosion she made she must have been full of mines, there was nothing left of her in three minutes. The blast gave us a good shaking up, but nobody minded as it meant another enemy ship less.'*

This was altogether a busy day, with an abortive attack on an escorted convoy just after midday, a patrol putting them under again at 2.15 p.m. 'with shots falling all around us' and a further alarm at 5.30 p.m. However at 6.45 they were able to have a little peace: 'we had a wash' says Haskins, 'the first in seven days and we certainly needed it'.†

Both the torpedoes fired at the convoy had either missed or failed to run properly. The 'heater' torpedoes carried by E 14 were the first of their type to be issued to submarines. They had an unfortunate habit of becoming partly defective if the tube, which had to be flooded when the torpedo was fired, was filled with water more than a very short time beforehand. Alterations of course by the enemy or other unforseseen delays meant a faulty run.

The precious torpedoes were indeed a frustrating weapon. Four days later E 14 fired at a laden transport escorted by a destroyer from point-blank range and watched the track of her torpedo running true towards the target. This time either the pistol failed or the torpedo ran deep. There was no explosion. 'The whole boat's crew (had) the blues' wrote Lawrence. But the presence of a British submarine on the sea-route from Constantinople was already having a considerable effect, with traffic to the peninsula being diverted to the much longer journey by rail and road.

The story of this first patrol inside the Sea of Marmara has to be read with a seeing eye. E 14 had kept her rendezvous with AE 2, and drew the correct deduction

* It was the Turkish *Nour-el-Bahr.*

† The designers of the E boats had not anticipated patrols lasting more than a few days. Little fresh water was carried. It was ten days before he again noted that he was "allowed a wash" when he must have needed it more than ever.

when Stoker failed to arrive. She was entirely alone, cut off from her friends by the difficult and dangerous Straits. The sea she was operating in was a small one, never more than 40 miles wide and not much over 100 miles long— not so large as the English Channel between the Isle of Wight and Dover. Change her position as she might her presence was constantly reported and the enemy had plenty of patrols at his disposal for such a limited area. She had only one serviceable periscope. If it, or any other vital fitting, was damaged, E 14 would not only be ineffective, but have no chance of eventually returning down the Straits. In the words of Boyle's own official report she was 'consistently harried by patrols'. Haskins' matter-of-fact account, with its laconic but frequent references to enemy ships appearing and putting them under, gives a better idea of the strain. At night, if the battery did not require charging, it was possible to dive to 60 feet, below the keels of any chance encounters, and relax, with a few men at 'watch diving stations'. The Marmara is very deep, up to over 700 fathoms, and there are not many shallows where a submarine can rest on the bottom. The technique of lying on the layer of denser salt water about 60 feet below the surface with both motors stopped had not yet been developed. Each day the battery had to be recharged, for periods varying between three and eight hours according to the use made of it.

It is not very easy for the reader, safe, comfortable and clean, to picture the rigours of a long cruise in a submarine in heavily patrolled enemy waters. Except when diving deep or resting on the bottom the crew is under constant strain. They live, eat and catch their sleep amongst the machinery, very occasionally allowed on deck in relays for a breath of fresh air and a glimpse of the sky. There is plenty to eat, but very limited cooking facilities, though a hot meal of sorts could be served once a day. Smoking is only allowed when on the surface with the diesel engines running to ventilate the boat. Dived there is a sort of chilly fug, which gradually becomes fouler as the hours go by and the oxygen in the air is used up. To be effective the patrol must be maintained for a long time. It is not a question of a few hours' tension, but of day following day. Beards sprout and everyone gets dirtier and dirtier, for water must be strictly rationed.

The heaviest strain is on the officers, and in particular the Captain. Not only is his a lone command in a sense which is rarely enjoyed by the captain of a surface ship; when the submarine is attacking his eye at the periscope is the only one that can see, so that everything depends on his judgement. Nowadays submarines have many devices to help them—sensitive listening gear, asdic, radar, underwater signalling apparatus. In 1915 the E boats had none of these things.

Neither had they anything but the most rudimentary devices for estimating the course and speed of the enemy they were attacking with their precious torpedoes. As with a shot-gun aimed ahead of a moving bird, it was largely a question of 'eye' if the long stalk was to be rewarded, if the torpedo ran straight, by a hit. For this reason torpedoes were usually fired at very short range, inside the area patrolled by escorting torpedo boats, with the submarine at periscope depth, within reach of their rams.

The diversion of traffic to the railroad route had thinned out the seaborne traffic, and on 8 May Boyle went right into the harbour at Rodosto in search of a target.

'We glided in slowly and waited half a mile from the shore' (wrote Lawrence.) 'People came running from all directions and soon a crowd had gathered.'

There was a very large steamer in port full of refugees from Gallipoli, which Boyle spared. Rifle fire was now opened from the shore, so E 14 made off, but the fact that an enemy submarine should behave in this fashion in broad daylight cannot have been without its effect. 'I expect the telegraph wires ashore were in a melting condition' says Lawrence.

The American consul in Constantinople, Mr Einstein,

provides an amusing postscript to E 14's visit to Rodosto. He learnt that the keeper of the Government stores reported that a submarine had entered flying the Turkish flag and had been supplied with petrol and other items before the truth was discovered—an ingenious way of balancing the books!

Two days later E 14 had better luck. The weather was perfect with maximum visibility and the submarine was lying on the surface. The sun was blazing down, the sea calm and there was nothing in sight, so Boyle allowed the hands not actually on watch to go overboard for a swim. They were blissfully splashing about in the clear, blue water, a wonderful treat for men who had not had their clothes off for nearly a fortnight, when a destroyer came over the horizon. Everyone clambered back on board and rushed, still naked to their diving stations. Later two transports appeared, escorted by another destroyer. The torpedo fired at the first transport missed, but a second torpedo hit the other transport. It was now evening and almost dark, but light enough to see a huge cloud of smoke rise up near the transport's foremast. It was the *Guj Djemal,* an ex-White Star liner of 5,000 tons, crowded with 6000 troops for Gallipoli and carrying a battery of field guns. This was an important success.

E 14 had now been in the Marmara for thirteen days. She had fired nine of her torpedoes and the only one left was defective, resisting all attempts by the ship's staff to put it right with the very limited means at their disposal.

The C.-in-C. sent his hearty congratulations, but ordered Boyle to remain on patrol. 'Moral effect of your presence invaluable.' The weather had broken and there was a spell of wind and rain, with a nasty, choppy sea. E 14's teeth were drawn, but the risks remained as before. On 13 May a steamer she was chasing opened fire with a small gun, hitting the conning tower with several shots, but luckily doing no vital damage. Next day Boyle gave orders for a dummy gun to be rigged on the casing in front of the conning tower, using a piece of pipe and an oil drum which, with the addition of some painted canvas, were converted into quite a convincing 'weapon'. Several ships were suitably impressed, stopping so that a boarding party could examine them. A small steamer took to her heels and ran herself ashore. That night, a particularly dark one, E 14 was surprised on the surface by a destroyer, and very nearly rammed. The roar of propellors passing immediately overhead was alarmingly audible. 'Our closest call' wrote Lawrence. As luck would have it, several transports passed within easy reach of E 14 during the next few days, her only remaining means of offence being a few rifle cartridges. Fresh water was now in very short supply, the crew being limited to a pint per man a day.

At 4.30 a.m. on 17 May, her twentieth day in the Marmara, she was at the western end reporting by wireless to Admiral de Robeck when she received orders to return, with a warning that anti-submarine nets had been reported off Gallipoli. Boyle had expected to be relieved in the Marmara by E 11. When Nasmith failed to arrive he made the obvious assumption.

He spent the rest of the day charging his battery and air bottles and getting everything ready for the passage down the Straits. During a quiet spell with nothing in sight he allowed the hands to bathe, for it was important that everyone should be at his best during the next few hours. Afterwards he dived to check the trim. No detail was ever forgotten in E 14.

At 7.30 a.m. on 18 May he approached Gallipoli on the surface, pursued by two old patrol craft which he was able to outdistance. There was no sign of the nets, but Boyle dived to 90 feet to pass below any obstruction. At noon E 14 was off Moussa Bank, approaching the really difficult part of the passage. Near Nagara, Boyle had the frustrating experience of passing within 400 yards of the old battleship *Toorgood Reiss,* unescorted and evidently quite unaware of his presence. At 1.30 p.m. he had safely rounded the awkward turn at Nagara and was in the Narrows, making good progress. To take full advantage of the fastest current Boyle remained at periscope depth, tailing a Turkish patrol boat which presumably knew her way through the minefields. He was not spotted until he was rounding Kilid Bahr where the forts opened fire. Boyle quietly dictated notes on the position of the guns before going deep to pass under the Kephez minefield.

An hour later E 14 was among the Allied ships off Cape Helles—not quite out of danger, for a French battleship, near which she rose to the surface, at first trained her guns on her. A minute later the Frenchmen were cheering as the white ensign was unfurled. A British destroyer arrived to escort her to Imbros. 'We had to go round the whole Fleet, and they certainly gave us a cheer,' remarks Haskins with satisfaction.

The cheers were well earned, for it had been an epic cruise. For twenty-one days E 14, alone since AE 2 was sunk, and entirely unsupported, had menaced the vital seaborne traffic between Constantinople and Gallipoli. One small vessel with a crew of thirty-seven had, in General Sir Ian Hamilton's words, been worth an Army Corps of 50,000 men. 'The Marmara is practically closed by English submarines,' wrote Mr Einstein from Constantinople a few days later. 'Everyone asks where their depot is, and how they are re-furbished.'

At Mudros E 14 had another tumultuous reception. As she secured alongside the depot ship Admiral Guépratte arrived in his barge, in which the French flagship's band had been embarked, leapt on board and kissed Boyle on both cheeks. He was a 'lovely boy' and all his crew were 'lovely boys'. Meanwhile the band played 'Tipperary' and 'God Save the King'. Equally sincere if less exuberant were de Robeck's congratulations, when Boyle dined with him that night. 'We were all thrilled by Boyle's simply told tale,' wrote the Chief of Staff, Roger Keyes, in his diary. Nasmith of E 11, whose departure up the Straits had been delayed so that he could benefit from Boyle's experience, was also at the Admiral's table. Later Boyle was having his first really undisturbed sleep for over a fortnight when he was aroused by a signalman. He had been awarded the Victoria Cross and all his officers and crew had been decorated.

The Turks had not seen the last of Boyle or of E 14. On the night of 10-11 June she again entered the Marmara for another successful patrol. She had been fitted with a little gun, a 3-pounder borrowed from one of the surface ships at Mudros. It was not a very lethal weapon, but useful for stopping the dhows and other small craft now carrying much of the traffic between Constantinople and the Gallipoli Peninsula because of the threat of British submarines. They were sunk by demolition charges after the crews had been removed, for the safety of merchant seamen was always a major consideration during this campaign. Lifeboats would be towed inshore or the crews embarked in the submarines and transferred to another vessel of no military value. 'Supplied wrecked mariners with rum and biscuits' is a typical entry in E 14's log. It was a strange experience for the Turks, but they took it all very philosophically.

This was in many ways a difficult patrol. The crew of a submarine is small, and every man valuable. Boyle and several others were suffering from a form of dysentry and were partly incapacitated. The First Lieutenant, Lieutenant Stanley, was very ill indeed. For some days he lay in his bunk, only semi-conscious and clearly at death's door. The thermometer in the submarine's medicine chest was broken and one of the large thermometers supplied for the battery gave the alarming reading of 106°F. Without expert attention Stanley might die, and Boyle was seriously considering stopping a Turkish hospital ship when his First Lieutenant began to recover.

After completing her full patrol of twenty-three days, E 14 passed down the Straits on 3 July. She surfaced off Cape Helles and anchored, ostensibly in safety. Suddenly a Turkish field gun opened fire and quickly found the range. Shells were falling very close, the capstan motor broke down, but Boyle escaped by going ahead on both engines, dragging his anchor behind him.

Just over a fortnight later he sailed again for the Marmara. The Turks, alarmed by the success of the British submarines, had been strengthening their defences and had laid two lines of 'deep' mines above Nagara. It had been reported that many of the large mooring buoys had disappeared from the Bosphorus and there were rumours of an anti-submarine net across the Straits.

Boyle, after passing up the Narrows for the third time, spotted a line of buoys above Nagara Point, but was able to slip through a gap or gate near the Asiatic shore.

Returning twenty-four days later he was less fortunate.

With his usual thoroughness he had thought out the technique he would use if he had to burst his way through. The line of buoys had not been quite at right angles to the current so he would adjust his course to meet the net exactly square. To ensure that E 14 remained horizontal after she struck he arranged that some of his crew should be prepared to run forward or aft as necessary —a much quicker proceedure than flooding or blowing tanks.

At full speed, with the current behind him, he hit the net. 'I was brought up from 80 feet to 45 feet in 3 seconds,' wrote Courtney Boyle in his report, 'but luckily only thrown 15 degrees off course. There was a tremendous noise; scraping, banging, tearing and rumbling . . . It took about 20 seconds to get through.' A few minutes later he was narrowly missed by two torpedoes fired from the fixed tubes at the Narrows, one of them breaking surface a few yards astern of the periscope. Passing under the Kephez minefield on the way up he had fouled a mine mooring which pulled E 14 dangerously off course and nearly cut through the jumping wire before it came clear. This time she again scraped past a mine: 'but it did not check me'. On surfacing outside it was found that the periscope standards, the bow and other parts were heavily scored by wires.

Boyle had now spent a total of 70 days in the Marmara. He was as cool and calm as ever, but perhaps his luck was beginning to wear a bit thin. E 14 had covered 12,000 miles without visiting a dockyard, a wonderful tribute to her crew in those day of rather unreliable machinery. She was sent to Malta for a refit and a well-earned rest.

CHAPTER FOUR

NASMITH AND E 11

LIEUTENANT Commander Martin Nasmith in E 11
sailed for the Straits on the night after Boyle in E 14
returned from his first patrol. He was off Cape Helles at
3.0 a.m., dived near Suandere to avoid the searchlights
and passed without incident under the Kephez minefield.
Following the example of E 14 Nasmith negotiated the
first part of the Narrows at periscope depth, but went
deep below Kilid Bahr. The current swept him close inshore and he grounded briefly in 54 feet of water whilst
rounding the point, but was soon off again. Rising for a
look round he was just in time to see the *Toorgood Reiss*,
reported by E 14 the day before, steaming away towards
Gallipoli, escorted by four destroyers, too far off for a
torpedo and going too fast to be overtaken. That night
E 11 surfaced in the western end of the Sea of Marmara.
The highly professional way in which Boyle and Nasmith
negotiated the Straits should not be allowed to disguise
the difficulties, which remained as before.

Boyle and Nasmith had joined the *Britannia* together
as cadets, were in the same gunroom as midshipmen in
the *Renown* (flagship of Sir John Fisher), volunteered for
submarines together, and had always been friends.
Nasmith was thirty-two years old. As a young Lieutenant
he had commanded one of the early 'A' boats. Just before
the war he held the key appointment of Training Officer
at Fort Blockhouse, the submarine depot, impressing his
own strongly-held ideas of the special qualities demanded
by the new Branch on the officers and ratings passing
through the school. In every type of surface ship there are
simple tasks which can be adequately performed under

supervision, but in submarines with their small crews every man held, to some extent, the lives of his shipmates in his hands. There was no place for the thoughtless, the slacker or the man who did not know his job. Thoughtlessness could not be guarded against by mechanical safety devices, and Nasmith believed that such fittings not only complicated design, but were positively dangerous, inducing a feeling of false security which might prove fatal. A submarine can be regarded as a single very complicated machine, its crew part and parcel of the mechanism, with which they must be entirely familiar. There was, perhaps, a trace of the fanatic in Nasmith, but his judgement was excellent, his grasp of his profession absolute and his courage of that entirely unflinching kind which is very rarely met with. In work as in play he had what a brother officer has described as a tendency to 'hold on to the ball too long', but the same observant contemporary adds a tribute to his remarkable strength of character and 'sheer love of battle'.* He had already distinguished himself in the North Sea before he came to the Mediterranean.

Next morning Nasmith started to hunt round for targets, but E 14's exploits had thoroughly alarmed the enemy and no shipping was seen. He turned east towards Constantinople.

So that he could remain on the surface unseen, he hit on the ingenious plan of capturing a small sailing vessel and lashing his submarine, trimmed down so that only the conning tower was above water, alongside. In this way E 11 spent 21 May in the Eastern Marmara, but the ruse did not meet with the success it deserved. That night he cast off and steered west again, was unsuccessfully attacked by a destroyer next day and returned to the Eastern Marmara during the night, on the assumption that patrols, summoned by the destroyer, would be hunting for him elsewhere. He had stopped and was searching a large sailing ship on the morning of his third day in the Marmara when he saw a big steamship steering for

* C. G. Brodie, *Forlorn Hope 1915*.

Constantinople. Recalling the boarding party, he was giving chase on the surface when he encountered the Turkish gunboat *Pelenk-i-Dria*. Nasmith dived and fired a torpedo, which hit, but the gunboat, gallantly shooting back as she was sinking, accomplished the almost impossible feat of hitting E 11's periscope with her very first shot, putting one of these two vital instruments completely out of action.*

E 11 spent next day in a quiet corner of the Marmara by the uninhabited Kalolimno Island draining, drying and plugging the now useless tube. All hands had a bathe and a breath of fresh air; the boat was cleaned and she turned towards Constantinople next morning refreshed, though with only one eye.

The first vessel they sighted was a small steamer. Nasmith, very conscious of only having such a limited supply of torpedoes, rose to the surface and forced her to stop by rifle fire, ordered her crew to abandon ship and prepared to board. The Turkish crew made off in haste, capsizing two of their three boats in the process though the sea was as calm as a mill pond. As E 11 came alongside a figure strolled on deck, introduced himself as Mr Raymond Gram Swing of the 'Chicago Sun' and said he was very glad to make their acquaintance. It was indeed that American journalist, who was to become so well-known in the 1939-45 war as a broadcaster over our own B.B.C.

Raymond Gram Swing had been on his way to Gallipoli, for the ship was carrying a small body of Turkish marines bound for Chanak. More important was her cargo, soon uncovered by the First Lieutenant of E 11, Lieutenant Guy D'Oyly-Hughes, and his boarding party —a six inch gun and its mounting, a number of lighter guns and a quantity of ammunition, which made a very satisfactory explosion when the demolition charges were fired. Being, of course, unable to take prisoners, Nasmith

* The top of E 11's periscope, almost severed by a ragged hole, can be seen in the Imperial War Museum.

allowed the crew to make off in their boats. In due course they returned to Constantinople to spread alarming tales, which Swing did nothing to contradict, of *eleven* British submarines loose in the Marmara to prey on shipping bound for Gallipoli.

E 11 next chased a steamer into Rodosto harbour, fired at her as she was securing alongside the pier and set her ablaze. The harbour was shallow and Nasmith kept on hitting the bottom. Turning into deeper water he sighted another steamer and surfaced to put a demolition party on board. The Turkish ship gamely attempted to ram, missed, made for the coast and ran herself ashore. E 11 closed with the intention of boarding, but had to desist when a cavalry patrol appeared and opened a brisk fire from the top of a nearby cliff. Again frustrated, Nasmith decided to use one of his precious torpedoes, but failed to score a hit. After this full but only partly successful day he retired for the night to charge his battery and to sit for a few hours on the layer of salt water which, as Boyle had now discovered, was conveniently disposed at a depth of sixty to ninety feet in many parts of the Marmara. Trimmed a few tons 'heavy' for the fresh water layer above, a submarine could sit suspended in the depths whilst all on board except a watchkeeper on the diving gauges had a rest.

Nasmith had now been 'up the Straits' for four days, but the bag was too light for his liking. Next morning he approached the coast on the surface until the domes and minarets of Constantinople were on the skyline, dived and proceeded into the entrance of the Bosphorus. Through his periscope he watched the Golden Horn, between the old city of Stamboul and the modern buildings of Galata and Pera, gradually opening up to port. A British submarine was in the very heart of the Turkish Empire.

The harbour was full of shipping anchored in the Bosphorus or secured alongside the wharves, but the larger Turkish warships were out of reach above the Galata swing bridge where the dockyard is situated.

Evidently an enemy warship was as unexpected as a U-boat in the Pool of London, for though it was as calm as a millpond E 11's periscope was not spotted. Passing close to the U.S.S. *Scorpion,* the American guardship, Nasmith looked for a suitable target. Alongside the arsenal, below the crowded hill on which Pera is built, was a Turkish gunboat. His first torpedo ran wild with a gyro failure, circling round at 40 knots and nearly hitting the submarine herself; but a second 'fish' sped straight towards the target. The sound of the explosion had scarcely died away when the first torpedo, which had darted under Galata Bridge, hit one of the wharves, throwing a great column of smoke and water into the air as the warhead exploded. The Turks, utterly dumbfounded, were at a loss to know what could have happened. Orders and counter-orders added to the general confusion as troops were hurriedly disembarked from transports waiting to sail. Rumours flashed through the streets of an invasion, shopkeepers put up their shutters; for several hours the normal life of the great city was brought to a standstill.

Meantime E 11, content with having stirred up a hornet's nest, turned to make her way back to the open sea. It was a tricky maneouvre in the strong current sweeping down the Bosphorus and she went aground, grating up a shelving underwater bank which brought her from seventy-five to forty feet before she came to rest. Stopping his motors Nasmith paused to consider the position.

What to do next depended on accurately determining where he was; on Seraglio Point by the old harem on the Stamboul side, or on the Leander Bank, off Skutari on the Asiatic shore. The two points were less than a mile apart and he could not be exactly sure of his position. The correct action to get off the European shore would drive E 11 still harder aground if she was in fact on the Asiatic side, and vice versa. As Nasmith considered the problem the helmsman reported that the submarine was pivoting slowly anti-clockwise in the current; she must therefore be on the eastern edge of the Bosphorus, off Skutari. Pinning his faith on having made a correct diagnosis Nasmith waited until E 11's bows were pointing up harbour and then went ahead with full port rudder. Scraping and bumping E 11 drew clear, turned south and passed without further incident into the Marmara. Next day he was again off Constantinople, but all sailings had been cancelled by the Turks and no shipping was moving. Nasmith calmly proceeded to photograph the mosques and minarets through his periscope, a photograph which was hanging in his cabin five years later when he returned to the Bosphorus as captain of the battleship *Iron Duke*.

E 11 had had a very full week and Nasmith felt that he and his crew would benefit from a short break. Withdrawing into the south-eastern Marmara they spent the next day cleaning ship, washing the clothes in which they lived and slept, bathing, making good small defects and relaxing in the sunshine under the lee of Kalolimno Island. In the early hours of 27 May E 11 was back on patrol, on the surface and keeping a sharp lookout, for it was a bright, moonlit night. Shapes appeared on the horizon which resolved themselves into a battleship (it was the *Barbarossa*) with an escort of destroyers. They would pass too far off for a torpedo attack so Nasmith decided not to dive until he had closed the range. Still unobserved he came closer, intending to press home his attack on the surface. But the battleship was still out of range when one of her escorting destroyers spotted him, turned to ram and was only just avoided by a very rapid 'crash' dive. Later that same day E 11 had another narrow escape when a yacht she had stopped and was about to board suddenly unmasked a gun and opened fire; probably the first 'Q' ship of World War I.

There was so little seaborne traffic in the northern Marmara that he turned south, entered the harbour of Panderma and torpedoed the merchant ship *Silivri*.

Six of his ten torpedoes had now been expended.

Nasmith was determined to keep one or two torpedoes for the warships he fully expected to find in the Dardanelles on his way out, so he had only three left for the week or more he intended to remain in the Marmara. Torpedoes are normally set to sink at the end of their run, if they fail to find a target, but Nasmith now ordered D'Oyly-Hughes to reverse this procedure, setting them to float as is done during torpedo practice. He was therefore able to recover the torpedo which missed a large storeship the following day, calmly rising to the surface after the ship had passed. It was a tricky operation, for the warhead was fully 'armed' and would explode if its whiskers were rapped. Bringing E 11 close to the torpedo Nasmith dived over the side, swam to the torpedo, and re-set the safety device (a miniature propeller on the pistol which locks the whiskers). The pistol was then removed and the torpedo hoisted onboard. It was struck below in the usual way, down the fore hatch. Whilst this was going on E 11 was unable to dive, so Nasmith, fearful of being caught on the surface with a hatch open whilst the torpedo was being slowly lowered inboard, decided that in future he would recover his 'fish' by trimming down until the stern tube was only just below the surface and sucking the torpedo, nose first, into the tube by running the ballast pump. By this ingenious means torpedoes could be recovered without robbing the submarine of her capacity to make an emergency dive.

On 31 May he torpedoed a supply ship in Panderma Roads which ran herself ashore with a heavy list, and on 1 June hit another ship which, judging by the force with which she disintegrated, must have been carrying ammunition. A smaller store ship, missed by a torpedo, beached herself in her consternation. Indeed E 11, appearing and disappearing now here, now there, was filling the Turks with alarm, fully convincing them that the reported flotilla of submarines was on their doorstep. But two nights later she was very nearly run down by a steamer as she lay on the surface off Constantinople. Nasmith crash-dived in a hurry and the steamer, thoroughly upset by the experience, turned about and returned to harbour. Next day a number of destroyers were sighted, apparently looking for E 11, but Nasmith was now down to his last two torpedoes so he contented himself by continuing to bob up in various places in the Marmara, rightly believing that by doing so the important merchant ship traffic to Gallipoli would be interrupted.

Unfortunately his engineers now reported a serious defect. A crack had appeared in one of the intermediate shafts between a diesel engine and its main motor. The main motor on the opposite side was a very doubtful quantity, with low insulation which gave a full brightness 'earth' on test. It was time to turn for home.

Nineteen days after he had entered the Marmara he was again off Gallipoli. Running deep down the first long leg he came to periscope depth as he neared Nagara. Two large merchant ships were anchored near the Asiatic shore off Moussa Bank, but Nasmith, after bigger game, rounded the point to look for warships in Kilia Liman. Boyle, returning without a torpedo, had seen plenty of targets there, but now there was nothing of importance in the anchorage.

Most men, after such a successful patrol, would have been content to continue down the Straits, but not Nasmith. Turning submerged, in narrow waters known to be mined and in a strong current which could very easily sweep him ashore, he returned above Nagara Point, sank the two empty merchant ships he had seen off Moussa Bank and finally turned for home. Nagara Point was again successfully rounded, but in the Narrows E 11 struck something which checked her momentarily. She was running deep at the time, but when she next came to periscope depth to fix her position, Nasmith observed a large black object surging along a few feet away—a mine whose mooring wire was evidently fast on some obstruction in the bows. Nasmith went deep and had another look. Through the clear water the nasty object was clearly visible, swinging from side to side on its fouled mooring about twenty feet away.

He decided that the safest thing to do was to remain deep, towing the mine above him, until he was clear of the Straits. Without mentioning what he had seen he continued as though everything was normal, though the next hour seemed a long one. When he judged he was out of gun-range and could safely show himself, he gave a number of surprising orders. Reversing his motors he blew the after ballast tanks, bringing E 11 to the surface down by the bow and with stern-way on. Through the periscope he watched the mine draw away ahead, and finally disengage its mooring wire from the forward hydroplanes with which it had become entangled.

Happy people have no history and submarines with unusually competent commanders seem marvellously free from tragic accidents. It is like watching the real expert playing a game; it all looks so easy, until you try to do it yourself.

This was the patrol for which Nasmith was awarded the Victoria Cross, but by no means the end of his adventures in the Marmara. Whilst E 11 was temporarily out of action at Mudros having her defects attended to, E 14 went in to take her place, followed during the next few weeks by two of the boats which had been sent from England to reinforce the flotilla: E 7 (Lt.-Comd. Cochrane) and E 12 (Lt.-Comd. Bruce). The French *Mariotte*, another new arrival, was less fortunate, running aground at 80 feet in the Narrows with her starboard propeller fast in some obstruction. In his efforts to get free, Lieutenant de Vaisseau Fabre broke surface, was hit by shell fire and sunk, though most of his crew managed to escape.

Ten days later Nasmith sailed for his second patrol, and his first attempt to pass the Nagara net. E 7, passing out a few days before, had 'burst through in fine style' without too much trouble, but the depth of the foot-rope at the bottom of the net, a virtually unbreakable 5 inch wire, varied with the strength of the current which was in turn affected by the weather conditions. E 11, diving along at 110 feet, hit the foot-rope, was almost brought to a stop, and came up 20 feet before the big wire slid down her stem with a loud crack, leaving it scraped and polished, but allowing her to burst safely through the smaller wires above.

Nasmith was not at all put out by this experience. Ten minutes after passing through the net he torpedoed and sank a transport lying in the Ak Bashi Liman anchorage. Next day he bagged a second transport which managed to get ashore stern first before she sank.

E 11 had been fitted with a 12-pounder gun. Floating targets were in short supply, so Nasmith, who had noticed troops passing down a road near Gallipoli in large numbers, spent the rest of the day bombarding them from the vicinity of a buoy which gave him an accurate range. (He had no range-finder.) He was finally put under by a field gun which 'opened a well-directed fire'.

The Suvla landings had taken place just before he entered the Marmara, threatening the enemy at a new point. Hard-pressed, the Turks decided to send the battleship *Harridin Barbarossa* to back up their artillery with her big guns. At 4.40 a.m. on 8 August Nasmith sighted her, with an escorting destroyer. Twenty minutes later he fired a torpedo, hitting the great vessel amidships. The battleship opened a heavy fire on E 11's periscope, but she was in serious trouble, listing to starboard and altering course towards the shore. She was still in deep water when Nasmith saw a great flash as though a magazine had gone up. Seconds later the *Harridin Barbarossa* rolled bottom up and sank. On 17 December 1914 Nasmith had fired a torpedo at a German battleship in the North Sea at a range of only 250 yards. The torpedo had dived under its target, and he had sworn he would give up tobacco until he had sunk a battleship. That night when E 11 surfaced to charge her batteries he was able to smoke his pipe.

The cruise continued to be full of incident. Targets worth a torpedo were scarce and Nasmith made full use of his gun. He was bombarding a steamer when the mounting fractured, throwing the gunlayer, Petty Officer John Kirkcaldy overboard: 'and the gun very nearly following him'. Picking up the gunlayer, Nasmith assessed the damage. It was considerable, but he was undismayed, finding a quiet spot where Chief E.R.A.* L. C. Allen and his staff succeeded in remounting the gun on a lower pedestal—quite a feat with such limited resources, and accomplished in twenty-four hours. Three days later he was bombarding the railway station at Mudania, scoring hits before being put under by fire from the shore.

After sinking a number of dhows by gunfire, first evacuating their crews, Nasmith tired of such small game, closed the mouth of the Bosphorus and observed a steamer alongside the railway pier at Haidar Pasha, the terminus on the Asiatic side. The steamer was behind a breakwater, but he ran up the harbour until the range was clear and torpedoed her. But the Turks were fighting back hard, and that evening he had a close call when a ship he was attacking suddenly opened a very accurate fire with a number of guns after pretending to be running for the shore. He spent the next day in the Gulf of Ismid, where the main railway line to Asia Minor runs close to the coast, and scored a number of hits on a viaduct. He then ran down to the western end of the Marmara to bombard the troops on the Gallipoli road from his usual position off the Dohan Aslan Buoy. During this trip Nasmith and D'Oyly-Hughes worked out a plan for a novel attack on the viaduct. The exploit which followed has often been described, but it is a story which bears repetition, for it is typical of the spirit animating E 11 and her crew.

In a quiet spot near Kalolimno Island they built a raft, using material taken from enemy ships. All hands had a swim whilst the raft was being tested. It was handy enough to be propelled by one man, but would support a

* Engine Room Artificer.

68

good sized demolition charge. That night, as the moon was setting, E 11 re-entered the Gulf of Ismid.

Near the viaduct they had bombarded was a cove surrounded by low cliffs which screened it from the landward side. Trimmed down so that only her conning tower was above water E 11 closed the shore at dead slow speed, grounding gently three yards from the beach. It was very dark and absolutely still, with a flat-calm sea. The raft was lowered over the side and Guy D'Oyly-Hughes, armed with a revolver and a sharpened bayonet and carrying an electric torch and a whistle, swam with it to the shore. Carrying the demolition charge he scrambled up the cliffs and made for the railway line.

It was a good deal further off than he had anticipated. After about half an hour he found the track, but his way to the viaduct was blocked by a patrol of three or four men, sitting by the line. In the stillness of the night he could hear them talking to one another.

Putting down the charge, which was heavy and cumbersome, D'Oyly-Hughes moved quietly inland, searching for another route. A small house loomed up ahead and a wall, over which he clambered, dropping into the middle of some roosting poultry. The resultant cackle was alarming, but the farmer must have been a sound sleeper for only D'Oyly-Hughes and the hens were disturbed.

He could now see the viaduct, still evidently under repair from the damage already inflicted by E 11. A big fire was burning, men were moving about, and a fussy little locomotive was letting off steam. Regretfully deciding that he could not fix the charge unseen he returned to the railway and began to search for another place where the line could be demolished. The only suitable spot was a small culvert, about 150 yards from the patrol. Pushing the charge under the track D'Oyly-Hughes muffled the fuse-pistol as well as he was able with a piece of rag, and pulled the trigger.

On so quiet a night the crack of the pistol was like a

cannon shot. There were shouts from the patrol as the
Turks leapt to their feet and began to run towards him.
D'Oyly-Hughes fired his revolver at the advancing men
and made off. Fortunately they paused to shoot back and
lost some valuable ground, allowing him to escape in the
darkness.

For some distance he ran down the line, where the
going was better, before turning seawards. The sounds of
pursuit had died away, but he was a long way from E 11
when he struck the beach. Perhaps Nasmith would hear
his whistle, but so would the Turks. Blowing it vigorously
he entered the water just as the charge exploded with a
highly satisfactory bang.

In the silence which followed D'Oyly-Hughes swam
steadily in the direction where he thought the submarine
must be. Day was not far off. He was very tired and there
was no sign of E 11. Returning to the shore he rested for
a while. After jettisoning pistol, bayonet and torch he
took to the water again, swimming wearily along the
coast. Something loomed up ahead, but it was a Turkish
rowing boat. Almost all-in, D'Oyly-Hughes turned for
the beach to hide among the rocks. He glanced back at
the Turkish boat, and discovered to his joy that it was
E 11's conning tower which he had mistaken in the half-
darkness. He had walked, run and swum a considerable
distance and was on the point of collapse when Nasmith
picked him up. As he was being hauled from the water
the Turks appeared on top of the cliffs, but E 11 'dived
out of rifle fire and proceeded out of the Gulf of Ismid'.

The next time Nasmith made contact with his Admiral,
outside the Straits, he was told that aircraft had reported
several transports at anchor above Nagara Point. He set
off immediately to look for them. To keep a full battery
he did most of the long 'leg' west from Gallipoli before
dawn, on the surface but trimmed well down. At daylight
he found the transports, with a destroyer and a gunboat
in attendance. Nasmith dived, and turned east, deliber-
ately showing his periscope occasionally to draw the

escorts after him. He then went deep and doubled back, torpedoed two large transports and fired at a third. Hearing no explosion he gave this ship another torpedo which hit by the foremast. She was 'last seen with her propeller revolving out of water'. During the afternoon he hit a fourth transport under the forecastle with his only remaining torpedo, and returned to the sea of Marmara after a most successful day.

Though now without torpedoes he had no intention of terminating his patrol, but continued to harry the enemy for a further thirteen days.

26 August   Overhauled and burnt small sailing vessel laden with grain. Washed clothes and cleaned out the Boat.

27 August   Dived into and carefully inspected Gulf of Mudania, but found nothing.

28 August   Rose to the surface at dawn and opened fire on Mudania Railway Station. Put under by shore guns.
                     10 a.m. Proceeded to attack by gunfire small steamer in the entrance to the gulf. She immediately however returned a sufficiently accurate fire to necessitate diving——Met E 2. Both boats carried out bombardment of Station and Magazine.

Nasmith's report of proceedings, written immediately after his patrols from entries made in logs and notebooks at the time, have a zest and sparkle which not even the staid official language can disguise.

On 31 August E 11 had a narrow escape when, operating close to Prinkipo Island, shore guns pitched a shell 'within yards of the after hydroplanes'. After bombarding his old friend the railway viaduct on the following day, and burning a couple of sailing ships after taking their crews on board for a while, Nasmith at last turned for home.

Having already proved that the first part of the journey down the Straits could be done trimmed-down on the surface, he came within eight miles of Nagara before diving, approaching the net with an almost full battery. On the previous day he had dismantled his gun and fitted an extra jumping wire. Guy D'Oyly-Hughes was stationed in the conning tower to observe what he could through the glass scuttles. It was 6.25 a.m. on a sunny day and a considerable amount of light penetrated even to 80 feet.

Nasmith approached at 'Half Speed—Grouper Up', but as soon as he felt the net he increased to full speed. E 11 checked, rose to 60 feet and then surged ahead with a snapping of wires. D'Oyly-Hughes, watching from the conning tower, reported (very accurately as it proved) a ten feet mesh 'of $2\frac{1}{2}$-inch wire crossed and securely joined'. E 11 proceeded on her way without any further incident.

But the net was a serious obstacle. As we learnt after the war it was up to 70 metres deep, extending from the surface to very near the bottom, with a mesh 9 to 12 feet square. It was kept in position by a number of large buoys moored to very heavy anchors. Between these buoys empty mine cases supported the head rope, and the foot rope was held down by sinkers. Searchlights, kept burning all night, lit the water above the net. Five motor gunboats patrolled the area, which was also covered by batteries of guns on shore. E 2 had been held up in it on her way to the Marmara on 13 August, fighting to free herself for ten minutes like a great fish and, when she at last broke clear, plunging to 140 feet before Bruce could regain control. E 7, going in to take E 11's place, charged the net at 100 feet, but picked up some of the wires with her starboard propeller. Robbed of half her power she swung broadside on to the net and was held there by the current. For three hours Cochrane tried to free himself, surging to and fro on his remaining shaft and altering his buoyancy. When these efforts failed he lay doggo, waiting for nightfall, intending to use the last of his compressed air to break away on the surface. The confidential books were destroyed and scuttling charges arranged to make sure that in any event she should not fall into enemy hands.

But the Turks had not been idle. It was still daylight when a tremendous explosion shook E 7, breaking lights and other fittings. The concussion might well have also damaged the net, and Cochrane made a last desperate effort to get clear. But he was still held fast. There was nothing for it but to surface and allow the crew to escape before sending E 7 herself to the bottom.

The Turks are a military nation. Their resources were not great, but they made the most of them. When Nasmith set out for his third Marmara patrol on 11 November there was much stiffer opposition to face. Extra minefields had been laid above the Nagara net, and near Suandere to catch the submarines before they dived, and there were now 16 lines of mines across the fairway. In the Marmara a number of the merchant ships were armed and guns had been mounted on shore to cover the places where the British submarines did most damage. More serious was the arrival of several U-boats, sent by the Germans to support their ally.

The destruction of E 7 had evidently badly damaged the net for in late September and early October E 12, H 1 (Lieutenant W. Pirie), E 20 (Lieutenant Commander Elkins) and the French Turquoise (Lieutenant de Vaisseau Ravenel) passed it without too much trouble. But the net had now been repaired and E 12, coming out on 22 October, had been very nearly destroyed when she picked up part of it around her bows and was carried down to 240 feet, well below her designed diving depth, before she broke clear with water spurting in from many leaks. The Turquoise, after twice running aground on her way up the Straits, had reached the Marmara with several defects and was in constant trouble with her very complicated and unreliable equipment after she had arrived. Forced to return to base (both periscopes were leaking, the gyro-compass out of action and the fore-

'planes almost unusable) she had run aground above Nagara and been captured before all the confidential papers had been destroyed.

The Turks had constructed a second net at Nagara below the old one. Nasmith avoided the new net, burst through the old one and passed on to above Gallipoli, expecting to meet E 20. But E 20 failed to arrive. A notebook left on board the *Turquoise* had given the time and place of an earlier rendezvous. UB 14 had kept the tryst, unrecognised as an enemy until it was too late. It was against this somewhat sombre background that E 11 began her third patrol. H 1 had completed her patrol and withdrawn and Nasmith was alone.

He did not know what had happened to E 20 but was aware that U-boats were about. Though not unduly put out by the additional risk, he had decided to work more at night, catching what rest he could with a branch from the bridge voicepipe laid on his pillow. Normal orders to the control room failed to wake him, but the least change of tone by the officer on the bridge would bring him from his bunk at once.

Patrols were active, but Nasmith reduced their number almost at once by sinking a destroyer with a torpedo which literally blew her into two pieces. The weather was bad, with frequent gales. The tops of the mountains in Asia Minor were covered with snow and it was extremely cold. Nevertheless he continued to dominate the Marmara. E 11 now had a 4-inch gun, a really useful weapon. In a fruitful patrol which lasted for 42 days she sank 11 steamers, 5 large and 30 small sailing vessels. As on his second patrol, the best 'bag' of larger ships was made by returning past Gallipoli to comb the anchorages above Nagara. Nasmith believed in keeping on the move, drawing the patrols to one point and then bobbing up in another. On 14 December he dived into the entrance of the Bosphorus and sank a ship alongside the jetty at Haida Pasha. A small tug fouled the range at the last moment, delaying the moment of firing so long that he ran aground with only 19 feet showing on the gauges as he turned to come out, but he extricated himself from this predicament with his usual skill. His narrowest escapes he only learnt about later, when enemy records were available after the war. Twice he was stalked by U-boats, one of whom missed him with a torpedo fired at close range. His strangest experience was in Panderma Harbour. E 2 had arrived in the Marmara to join E 11. Before the war she had been fitted with a periscope made in Germany. E 11 was diving out of Panderma after looking for targets when Nasmith saw a German periscope 200 yards on his beam. Thinking it belonged to E 2, he took no action, but learnt later that Bruce had been elsewhere at the time.

It is sometimes alleged, by the recipients of Britain's highest honour, that the award of the Victoria Cross is a matter of 'luck'—of being in the right place at the right time and of being *known* to be there'. If any proof was needed to dispel this illusion it is found in the story of E 11. It is a tale not only of dangers cheerfully found and constantly overcome, but of an aggressive spirit, continuously applied over very long periods, which yielded results which lesser men will freely admit as being quite beyond their capabilities.

Early in December the Allied Governments had decided to evacuate their troops from Gallipoli, an operation which was carried out on the nights of 18th and 19th. On 22 December, E 11 prepared to return down the Straits, rigging the special net-cutting gear which Nasmith had evolved. Next day she proceeded on the surface past Gallipoli, dived off Burgas Bay, burst through the new net at Nagara and rose to the surface for the last time off Cape Helles, now in Turkish hands. This third patrol had lasted 47 days. E 2 followed her out on 3 January.

In a campaign of just over eight months nine submarines had passed up the Straits, E 11 and E 14 three times, E 2 and E 12 twice. Four British and three French submarines had been sunk, either in the Straits or in the

Marmara—a high proportion of casualties, which fortunately did not include the whole of their crews. The submarines sank 2 battleships, a destroyer, 5 gunboats, 9 transports, 30 steamers, 7 ammunition and supply ships and 188 smaller craft. Seaborne traffic through the Marmara was reduced to a trickle. The enemy was forced to divert much of his limited resources to retaliation, using U-boats, guns, mines and personnel which were badly needed elsewhere. Indeed the effect of the submarines, if not quite decisive, was certainly considerable. By modern standards the military resources devoted to this very successful submarine campaign were small—economy of effort in a classic form.

CHAPTER FIVE

SANDFORD AND C 3

IN 1917 Allied merchant ship losses reached the staggering total of nearly four million tons. Even its staunchest supporters would never have claimed, in 1914, that the submarine would be producing results which were very nearly decisive only three years later. 1942, when the U-boats so nearly succeeded in winning the Battle of the Atlantic, and the war, is comparatively recent history. The fact that a similar crisis arose in World War I is sometimes forgotten. On land the war was also going badly and the future was exceedingly dark.

Many of the submarines preying on shipping in the Channel and Western approaches were based in Flanders, passing to and from their patrol positions through the Straits of Dover. Roger Keyes, now a Rear-Admiral, was appointed in command of the Dover Patrol. As he tackled with his usual vigour the problem of denying the Straits to the enemy, he was working on a plan to immobilise the main U-boat base, at Bruges, by blocking its access to the sea through the canals leading to Zeebrugge and Ostend.

The attack on Zeebrugge, on St. George's Day, 1918, has often been described. The essence of Keyes's plan was to sink blockships in the mouth of the canal, a point protected by numerous batteries on the coast and on the great crescent-shaped mole, over a mile long, which forms the artificial harbour at Zeebrugge. To reach the canal the blockships would have to pass very close to the mole. They would have little chance unless the guns on the mole could be captured or at least heavily engaged by a diversionary attack, drawing the enemy's fire from the main objective. But the mole was strongly fortified and well garrisoned. The number of men which could be landed on it by assaulting craft was limited and it was essential to prevent the Germans bringing in reinforcements as the attack developed. How could this be done?

For most of its length the mole is a concrete structure eighty yards wide, virtually impossible to destroy. But the strong tides which sweep the Belgian coast would soon have silted up the harbour if the shoreward end of the mole had been continuous, so the mole proper was joined to the coast by a viaduct built on iron piers. If this viaduct could be breached the mole would be isolated.

Keyes has told us that his first idea was to float rafts laden with high explosive against the piers, but one of his staff officers, Lieutenant-Commander F. H. Sandford, D.S.O., now had a much better plan. Why not use an old submarine, its bow crammed with high explosive? A submarine with its low silhouette would stand a chance of getting fairly close unobserved; even on the surface most of its vitals were below the waterline, and its shape was ideal for penetrating between the piers of the viaduct, forcing its forepart right under the forty-foot wide structure it was aimed to destroy.

Keyes at once agreed. One submarine would be sufficient, but two would be used, in case of accidents. C1 and C3 were made available; old vessels rather similar to the B class and of little military value at this stage of the war. Even more important was the question of their crews. All who attacked Zeebrugge on that St. George's Day faced great hazards, but the chances of the submarines, approaching a strongly defended point at comparatively low speed, without any means of offence to make the enemy keep their heads down, were clearly pretty slim.

The odds against getting there, and coming away alive, were slender, but there was no lack of volunteers. From those who came forward unmarried men were selected. Lieutenant A. C. Newbold would command C1 and Lieutenant R. D. Sandford, one of Commander Sandford's younger brothers, C3.

Richard Douglas Sandford, the seventh son of the Archdeacon of Exeter, was twenty-seven years old. He had joined the Navy as a cadet in 1904, volunteered for service in submarines ten years later and had been in 'The Trade' for the whole of the war—a cheerful, competent young man with a mock-old manner, he was generally known as 'Uncle Baldy'. As a member of a large family with a strong tradition of public service his sense of duty was as natural as breathing, but there was nothing smug or self-satisfied about him. His happy, humorous outlook on life was contagious. The world, to Dick Sandford, had always seemed a jolly place, and when he was around it became so. Though normally quiet and gentle he was exceedingly determined. Though never much of a talker, he got things done. Indeed, if past form was anything to go on he was exactly the man for the job.

Each submarine would carry a crew of six, two officers and four ratings. 'Stout-hearted and enterprising men', in the words of the official letter calling for volunteers. In C3 with Sandford were Lieutenant John Howell-Price, D.S.C., R.N.R. as navigator and second-in-command, Petty Officer Walter Harner, the Coxswain, Leading Seaman William G. Cleaver, Engine Room Artificer Allan G. Roxburgh and Stoker Henry Bindall. The meticulous preparations and very careful planning which were essential for success now began.

Fortunately detailed drawings of the viaduct were available from refugees from Belgium, engineers who had been concerned in its construction. Up-to-date aerial photographs showed any more recent alterations. The heavy timbers carrying double railway lines to the mole rested on a steel framework supported by tubular iron piers, six in a row across the viaduct's width. These piers, sixteen and a half feet apart, were cross-tied to one another. A very important feature was a strong horizontal girder running lengthways between the piers 16½ feet below the top. At high water, when the attack would take place, this horizontal girder would be about ten feet below the surface. The stem of a cigar-shaped submarine would clear this girder and burst through the cross-bracing above. As the bow ran under the viaduct the keel would ride up on the girder, whilst the conning tower would prevent the submarine going too far through. Five tons of amatol stowed well forward should be very nicely placed for its work.

So far so good, but the crews must be given some chance of escape before the charge, fired by a time-fuse, went off. Each submarine would tow two motor skiffs. Gyro steering gear was fitted so that the submarines could be abandoned a short distance before they rammed their objective, an ingenious paddle-controlled switch preventing the time-fuse from operating whilst the submarine was still moving through the water. The skiffs might be damaged or destroyed during the approach under fire and the crews might still be on board when the submarines struck.

Each submarine carried two light scaling ladders. If they were very lucky the crews could still escape by climbing the viaduct and making their way to our assaulting ships alongside the mole, using a narrow ledge which ran along its seaward side. There would be five minutes after the fuse was fired in which to get away. Yes, there was a chance.

The destruction of the viaduct was, of course, only a part of the plan for the blocking of Zeebrugge, one piece of the elaborate organisation in which no less than seventy-five vessels large and small would eventually take part. At the end of March 1918 all was ready.

Surprise was the essence of the plan and the Belgian coast, one of the most strongly fortified areas in the world, could only be approached under cover of darkness. Night alone was not a sufficient cloak and an on-shore wind was also essential. Numerous small craft would precede the main attacking force, laying a blanket of artificial fog or smoke on both sides of the harbour and blanking out the flanking coastal batteries, though the harbour itself must be left clear.

On 11 April the attacking force was foiled by a last-minute change of wind, and had to turn back when only thirteen miles from its objective. Two days later Keyes was again frustrated, this time by a rising sea which would have made it impossible for his assault ships to lie alongside the mole. The effect on the men engaged, keyed up for such a desperate venture and then reprieved, can be imagined. Twice the great armada of ships had sailed and twice returned, and the Admiralty almost decided at this point that the enemy must have got wind of what was afoot. Keyes pleaded to be allowed to try again and got his way, though the conditions would now be less favourable with moonlight thinning the darkness. In so far as the submarines were concerned the false starts had one advantage, disclosing that the rescue skiffs could not be towed without damage, and arrangements were made to hoist them on board.

At 2.0 p.m. on 22 April C 1 and C 3, each in tow of a destroyer, left Dover once again. A third destroyer towed a steam picket boat commanded by Lieut-Commander F. H. Sandford. The picket boat would accompany the submarines, hide them during the final stages of the approach by laying smoke, and try to rescue the crews.

At 5.0 p.m. the whole great force had assembled and was on its way, steaming at 10 knots. Except for an awkward swell the sea was calm. A light breeze blew from the north-east. All promised well as the day ended and darkness fell.

At ten o'clock the force was about fifteen miles from Zeebrugge. So far the enemy had given no sign of realising that anything unusual was afoot. Most of the ships were disposed in three columns, the centre headed by the *Vindictive* which was acting as the guide of the fleet, leading it past the buoys which had already been laid along the line of advance to ensure the absolutely accurate navigation necessary. C 3, wallowing along behind the destroyer *Trident,* was in the starboard column. To port Sandford could see the dark shape of *Vindictive* towing the smaller assault ships, *Iris* and *Daffodil.* Astern the destroyer *Mansfield* with C 1 in tow dipped and curvetted in the swell. Astern of her was the destroyer *Phoebe,* towing the picket boat commanded by his brother.

At 10.30 p.m. the starboard column altered course, inclining away from the *Vindictive's* column towards the shore. The motor launches and coastal motor boats which were to lay the smoke screens vanished into the darkness ahead. Everything had been so well rehearsed that very few signals were necessary. On deck all was dark. In the conning positions below men looked at their charts and watches.

Two things happened at about this time. The tow rope between *Mansfield* and C 1 parted. The long swell which had caused the trouble was making life difficult for the picket boat which was towing very badly and becoming almost impossible to control. As the picket boat yawed from side to side, the suddenly tightened tow-rope pulled her on to her beam ends. If the rope had not carried away she would have capsized None of this was known by Sandford in C 3.

At 11.20 p.m. diversionary raids by aircraft and a covering bombardment by monitors offshore were due to begin. A light, misty rain was falling and the wind had become fitful. Ashore in England the mist was much thicker, keeping our aircraft on the ground. Out at sea the mist was worrying the monitors, and their guns were still silent. *Vindictive* and her force had reduced speed to 6 knots. It was very quiet. A shaded light flashed a signal and C 3 slipped her tow rope. It was 11.26 p.m., the exact moment scheduled.

Now there was a hitch. With so many vessels working in a comparatively small area, movements had been carefully worked out in advance. Four minutes had been allowed for C 3, C 1 and the picket boat to assemble. When the others failed to materialize out of the darkness astern Sandford carried on alone. It was essential to stick to the plan. At 8½ knots he steered on the first leg of the course which should bring him to the viaduct.

Admiral Keyes had explained to his Commanding Officers not only what they should do, but what their neighbours would be doing. All sorts of other ships were around—motor launches, coastal motor boats, destroyers— but it was a dark night and nothing could be seen but the inky water rustling by, the dim sky overhead and C 3's wake gleaming astern. The six men and their little submarine were very much alone. It was a comfort when brightness flickering along the horizon on their port quarter showed that the monitors were at last in action, though fifteen minutes late. Bombardments by monitors were a regular occurrence. There was no reason why this one should alarm the enemy unduly.

At ten minutes to midnight C 3 was nearing the line of the smoke-making craft ahead. *Vindictive*, as Sandford knew, must now be approaching the mole. There was still no sound from the enemy, but his reaction, which would surely be violent, could not now be long delayed. A minute later C 3 altered course slightly to port and increased speed to 9½ knots. This was the last leg of the approach. It was to bring her, eleven minutes later, to her objective: 'Collision with the viaduct should take place', said the orders.

Suddenly a star shell gleamed in the void overhead, flared into white flame and began to drop slowly seaward. Others quickly followed it. Where all had been darkness it was soon bright with an eery white light. Seconds later big shells began to rumble by overhead from the heavy guns on the coast. They passed with a roar like a train, to fall somewhere far out at sea. Clearly the Germans were laying down a barrage to keep the monitors at a distance. There was still no sign that they suspected what was happening much closer at hand.

2355. *Vindictive,* due alongside at midnight, must be very near the lighthouse at the end of the mole. They *must* see her soon. Thicker darkness ahead of C 3 marked the edge of the smoke. Now it was wreathing round the submarine, evil-smelling stuff. The breeze from the north-east had been replaced by a little wind from the *south.* The smoke was thick enough here, but it was blowing not towards the shore, but out to sea.

C 3 was still hidden when a tremendous cannonade opened up somewhere not far away on her port hand. Sandford could distinguish nothing, except the flashes of gunfire and the glare of explosions. Above the smoke which still shrouded him the sky seemed to be as bright as noonday.

Vindictive, revealed by the northward-blowing smoke, was running the gauntlet at full speed. Badly battered and with heavy casualties she reached the mole. It was one minute after midnight.

At almost the same moment C 3 emerged from the smoke. According to the plan the viaduct should be quite close, but because of the shift of wind it was still about a mile and a half away, ten minutes steaming instead of only two or three. Shells cracked into the water nearby. There was no picket boat to lay a temporary screen. Sandford switched on his own smoke-making apparatus, but the cloud blew uselessly to seaward. C 3 was quite alone, and very much exposed. It seemed impossible that she could reach the viaduct without being sunk, but the shell fire suddenly ceased. Surprised but grimly thankful, Sandford held on.

With half a mile to go a great flare inside the harbour silhouetted the black mass of the mole on his port hand. For a moment mole and viaduct were clearly visible. Sandford made a slight adjustment to his course and ordered his crew to come on deck. He had no intention of trusting to the gyro-steering gear, but there was nothing more to do below.

Two hundred yards to go! This unhindered approach,

made with a great battle in full swing half a mile away, was strange and eery. 'A silent and a nervy business' said Stoker Bindall later. What could the enemy be up to? C 3's little crew, clustered by the conning tower, could hear men talking and laughing on the viaduct. Search-lights flashed on, blinding them momentarily, but were switched off again. (It seems that the Germans thought C 3 had lost her way and was trying to enter the harbour. It would be a fine thing to lure her on and catch a British submarine alive!)

Crash! C 3's bow hit the cross-braces exactly half way between three rows of piers. Steaming at full speed and with the current behind her she ran up on to the hori-zontal girder exactly as they had hoped, coming to rest with her bow right under the viaduct. Telling his crew to lower the skiff. Sandford lit the fuse.

But now the Germans seemed suddenly to realize what was intended. Searchlights blazed down. Rifles, machine guns and pom-poms stuttered into action. As the skiff was lowered it was hit several times. The six men tumbled aboard. The engine was started, but the current, running eastward through the viaduct, swept the boat on to C 3. The whirling propeller hit the submarine's exhaust pipe. The engine coughed to a stop; it was useless.

Half their precious five minutes had gone. It was certain death to be caught on the viaduct or in the water when five tons of amatol exploded. Bindall and Harner each seized an oar, straining desperately to move the heavy skiff against the current. She had been holed in several places. Water welled up round their feet. Luckily special bilge pumps had been fitted which just kept it at bay. Bindall was knocked out, but Cleaver grabbed his oar. Now Harner was hit. Roxburgh took his oar as Price hauled the two wounded men out of the way into the bows. Sandford, at the tiller, was hit and hit again. Price scrambled aft to take his place.

The skiff, stemming the current, had not gone far when there was a tremendous explosion. A pillar of flame soared

into the sky. Debris, flung high from the breached viaduct, shot upwards and began to fall. Great lumps of
metal smashed into the water all round the little boat,
miraculously missing it.

The explosion, in addition to blowing a hole 100 feet
long in the viaduct, had severed the power supply to the
searchlights and damaged telephone wires between the
mole and the shore batteries. Gunfire died down as the
skiff, with half her crew badly wounded, struggled out to
sea.

All this time F. H. Sandford in the picket boat had been
steaming at full speed towards the viaduct, trying desperately to come to the aid of C 3. To his delight he now
sighted the skiff and ran quickly alongside. The six men
were taken aboard. Dick Sandford, Harmer and Bindall
were badly wounded, in need of immediate attention
beyond the resources of the picket boat's crew. Fortunately
the destroyer *Phoebe,* who carried a doctor, was not far
away. Indeed their lucky star was in the ascendant that
night, for although the *Phoebe* was one of the last ships to
leave Zeebrugge after the attack and was still in action
an hour later, rescuing the crew of another destroyer sunk
in the harbour, they were safely back in Dover next day.

Each of the four ratings was decorated with the C.G.M.,
Howell-Price received the D.S.O. and Dick Sandford was
awarded the Victoria Cross. In bed in hospital recovering
from his wounds Sandford received the news with his
usual modest charm. 'Well done Uncle Baldy' telegraphed
one of his many friends.

Sandford was out and about again three months later,
but the almost miraculous good fortune which had
favoured him on St. George's Day seemed to have deserted
him. On 23 November 1918, twelve days after the
armistice had been signed, this cheerful, faithful, courageous man died, a victim not of the enemy but of
typhoid fever. His portrait hangs in a place of honour in
the officers' quarters at Fort Blockhouse. Like the man

it represents there is nothing flamboyant about it, but the artist has captured something very valuable to hand down to Dick Sandford's successors—a glimpse of a simple, steadfast soul.

CHAPTER SIX

WHITE AND E 14

WITH the war in its fourth year the battle-cruiser *Goeben** and the cruiser *Breslau** still threatened traffic in the Eastern Mediterranean. Powerful, modern and fast they could have caused havoc, were they to issue from the refuge in the Sea of Marmara which they had gained in August 1914. With the passing of time the ships assembled within reach of their only exit, the Dardanelles, had been reduced both in quality and quantity. Would *Goeben* and *Breslau* ever come out? It seemed increasingly doubtful. By Christmas 1917 the heavy ships on the Allied side consisted only of the old pre-Dreadnought battleships *Lord Nelson* and *Agamemnon*, supported by light forces, but the area off Gallipoli had been extensively mined. A destroyer patrol was maintained off Imbros, but it was dull work.

Then, on 20 January 1918, the unexpected happened. *Goeben* and *Breslau* passed down the Dardanelles in the darkness, unreported and unobserved. Not far from Cape Helles *Goeben* struck a mine, but the German ships were very well constructed against underwater damage and neither her speed nor her efficiency was affected. As daylight was coming the two ships arrived off Pyrgos, brushed off the attempts of two patrolling destroyers to stop them and began to bombard Kusu Bay as the alarm signal was being passed. Two monitors, the *Lord Raglan* and the *M 28*, at anchor in the harbour, were sunk before they had fired a shot. The raiding force turned north-west

* Officially part of the Turkish Navy, but still manned by German crews, the *Yawuz Sultan Selim* and *Midilli* are best referred to by their original names.

88

towards their primary objective, Mudros, where a considerable number of ships was assembled. There was nothing between the raiders and an important success except the *Agamemnon,* too slow to intercept them if they wished to avoid action. The *Lord Nelson* was many miles away at Salonika. Luckily for the Allies, enemy information about the exact position of the minefields was poor. Shortly after leaving Pyrgos *Breslau* ran into trouble, striking a mine and coming to a standstill. *Goeben,* whilst trying to take her in tow, also hit a mine. *Breslau* now struck four or five more mines and began to sink and the German admiral decided he must leave her to her fate and withdraw to the Dardanelles. He entered the Straits and passed up the Narrows without further incident.

Goeben was still an effective fighting ship, but she had several compartments flooded and was deep in the water. Rounding Nagara Point she ran aground. There is virtually no rise and fall of the tide in the Dardanelles and all efforts to re-float her were at first unsuccessful.

The Allies were, to put it mildly, exceedingly put out by the events of the day. True, the *Breslau* had been sunk, but two British monitors had been lost and the *Goeben* had once more escaped. Air reconnaissance flown from Mudros and Imbros reported the predicament of the *Goeben,* but she was beyond the reach of any surface ships. Every available aircraft was pressed into service and, during the next few days, no less than 270 sorties were flown over her. The aircraft of those days could only carry small bombs, but large numbers were dropped. Sixteen direct hits were claimed and it was confidently believed that the *Goeben* had been seriously damaged.

But such reports were far too nebulous. It was essential to make sure that the *Goeben* was completely immobilised. The Commander-in-Chief decided to send a submarine up the Straits to finish her off.

No submarine was immediately available, for E 12, attached to the Dardanelles patrol, was out of action with machinery defects. At Malta nearly 1000 miles away E 2 was just completing a dockyard refit; one of her two bow torpedo tubes was still out of action. The nearest fully effective submarine was at Corfu; E 14, one of the boats employed patrolling the Straits of Otranto. On 22 January she was passing through the Corinth canal on her way to the Dardanelles.

Since Boyle had negotiated the Straits in 1915 all E 14's officers and senior ratings had been replaced by other men. Her new crew was a good one, but had no experience of the difficult Dardanelles. The situation had altered radically in other respects. Surface patrols were now armed with effective depth-charges. Sensitive hydrophones had been developed which could pick up a submerged submarine at a considerable distance. Large numbers of guns, covering the waters of the Straits, were still in place, and additional minefields had been laid. In the words of the official Naval Historian, the 'obstructions off Chanak (were) far more formidable than they had been in the early days of the Dardanelles campaign'. Immediately after the return of the *Goeben* on 20 January a minelayer had been observed putting down yet another field between Cape Helles and Kum Kale. The Straits were exceedingly well defended.

On 24 January three submarines had been assembled; E 14, E 2 newly arrived from Malta, and E 12, which had rectified the more important of her defects. It was clear, however, that neither E 2 nor E 12 was in the necessary state of maximum efficiency which would give a chance of success.

The Commander-in-Chief, Vice-Admiral A. Calthorpe knew that E 14 had a well trained and experienced crew, and he was greatly impressed by the fine spirit of her commanding officer, Lieutenant Commander Geoffrey Saxton White. 'A more devoted officer', as he wrote later 'could not have been found for such a dangerous task'. Calthorpe was under no illusions about the hazardous nature of the enterprise. Neither was White. At a conference aboard the flagship where the operation was discussed in detail he listened calmly to the facts and quietly announced that he thought he could get through to Nagara. No submarine had been up the Straits for over two years and surprise would be on his side. Whether he could get down again after raising a hornet's nest was another matter and best not mentioned.

Geoffrey White, born in Kent, had volunteered for submarines as a lieutenant in the early days of 'The Trade'. He had served in one of the 'A' boats and had commanded C 27 before the war. In 1913 he was promoted to Lieutenant Commander and he was doing his 'big ship time' in the battleship *Monarch* when war was declared. In 1915 he returned to submarines to command D 6, one of the Harwich flotilla working in the North Sea. In 1916 he was sent to the Mediterranean to take over the famous E 14 from Commander E. C. Boyle V.C., an old friend. He had married in 1910 and had two small sons. The Whites' third child, a daughter, was born after he left England. Geoff White, thirty years old, was a strong, thick-set, quiet, competent and very modest man. He was an excellent submarine C.O., experienced and considerate. He and his crew had been together for some time, and mutual confidence was strong. Two days were spent making final preparations. The possibility that E 14 might be salvaged by the enemy after being sunk was squarely faced, and all the confidential books were transferred to the depot ship. Whilst this was going on White was flown over the straits in a seaplane. The *Goeben* was still in the same position, just below Nagara Point, with her bows fast on a shoal. If E 14 could negotiate the minefields and pass up the Narrows there would be a good chance of torpedoing her with a beam shot from a position near the European shore. But the waters in which E 14 would have to manoeuvre were narrow and heavily patrolled. The fire which greeted the seaplane left no doubt that the defences were thoroughly on the alert.

White, in consultation with Commander K. M. Bruce, who was in general charge of the operation, decided that the numerous surface patrols made it impracticable to attempt to pass up the Dardanelles in daylight, as had been usual in 1915. This added greatly to the navigational difficulties, fully explained in earlier chapters, but the only chance of success lay in taking the enemy completely by surprise. Heavy attacks by British aircraft would be made on the *Goeben* just after daylight. It was hoped by this means to divert attention whilst E 14 made her final approach up the Narrows. Immediately after the air attacks White would press home his torpedo attack. Timing of such accuracy would be difficult to achieve, and he might be in some danger from our own bombs, but this was accepted. Admiral Calthorpe's wording of his report, that the operation was 'an exceedingly hazardous matter' was certainly no exaggeration.

On 27 January bad weather prevented any flights over the *Goeben* until about noon, when she was observed lying in her usual position. Thick cloud prevented the usual air attacks that day, but during the night the skies cleared, promising a fine day on 28 January, the day fixed for E 14's attempt.

White sailed from Imbros at 5.0 p.m. on 27 January, as the short winter's day was closing down. Conscious that everything had been done which could ensure success, he was quietly confident. He could not know that, through an error in staff work for which he bore no responsibility, the fact that a British submarine would be in the Straits had not been communicated to all of our own patrols.

E 14 closed the entrance to the Straits, running on the surface on her diesel engines to save the battery. British lookouts on Mavro Island sighted her, mistook her for a U-boat, and signalled an alarm. The alarm was cancelled, but the original message had gone out over the air, to friend and foe alike.

To avoid the new minefield between Cape Helles and Kum Kale, White stopped his diesel engines short of its reported position, dived, and went to 100 feet. The loom of the land had been discernible from the bridge, but it was after 10.0 p.m. and pitch dark. Nothing could be seen through a periscope; he would have to rely entirely on dead reckoning for navigating the long first leg under the Kephez minefield to Sari Siglar Bay.

As dawn was lightening the sky over Asia Minor flights of aircraft took off, crossed the dark shape of the Gallipoli Peninsular and swooped down on Nagara for their attacks. Anti-aircraft guns flashed on both shores. In the growing light the winding ribbon of the Straits was clearly visible, but there was no sign of the *Goeben*. What had happened? Further reconnaissance flights during the day confirmed that the *Goeben* was nowhere in the Straits. Where was she, and where was E 14?

Shortly after 11.0 a.m. an aircraft flying over the lower Straits sighted something which the observer thought might be a submarine. Puffs of smoke on shore and white feathers springing up on the sea showed that the batteries were in action. The aircraft could not see exactly what was happening, but reported that gunfire continued for some time. When the submarine—if that was what it was—was off Kum Kale what appeared to be an explosion was observed; a rapidly growing circle of disturbed water around her. After this there was nothing on the surface, but a streak still seemed to be moving from the neighbourhood of the lighter-coloured water towards the open sea. It was imprecise, unsatisfactory information, but when the short winter's day ended and there was still no word from E 14 it looked like bad news. Further flights over the Straits had nothing significant to report.

White had dived at about 9.30 p.m. the night before. To keep below the Kephez minefield he ran along at 100 feet, occasionally coming to periscope depth to try and check his position. In the darkness it was exceedingly difficult to pick out any marks on shore. Several times, when running deep, scrapings along the hull indicated that he was in the minefield, and the absence of any surface craft confirmed the supposition. White went deeper, to 150 feet. After this the scrapings ceased.

At about 5.30 a.m. he reckoned he must be above the Kephez minefield and came to periscope depth. It was still dark, but there were cliffs or high land to port and low lying land to starboard. White decided he was just below the Narrows, went down again to 150 feet and increased speed. Shortly afterwards he rose to periscope depth for another look round. He was trying to fix his position when he found that E 14 was no longer moving past the shore. There had been no shock or scrape of grounding; she was caught in some invisible obstruction. With the current still sluicing past at about three knots she continued to answer to her hydroplanes and rudder and remained under control.

It was still dark, but light enough to see that there were no patrols in the vicinity, so White rose cautiously to the surface. He could now go astern, but it was no use; E 14 was firmly held.

To say that she was in an awkward predicament is a monumental understatement. At any moment she might be sighted, either by a patrolling ship or from the shore. Searchlights would reveal her to the batteries under whose guns she lay. Dived she might escape notice, but it was useless to dive without knowing the nature of the obstruction and how best to get clear.

Telling his First Lieutenant to take over, and to submerge instantly if an emergency arose, White went up the conning tower hatch alone. On the bridge he could see better, but still could not make out what was holding his submarine. Calling up a man to stand by the voicepipe and pass orders, he climbed down on to the casing and walked quickly into the bow. A shout from him would cause the main vents to be opened; E 14 would be under water again in a matter of seconds. White would be left in the water, and in the strong tide and darkness his chances of being picked up were negligible, but he calmly accepted this risk.

Alone on the bow, with the water sluicing by, he was able to pass the necessary orders which got his submarine clear. Without being seen E 14 again dived, and went to 100 feet. White had seen the two marker buoys which might indicate the position of a channel through the Narrows minefield. 'Luck was with us' remarked the coxswain, Petty Officer Robert Perkins, when describing the incident later.

Dawn was not far off when White cleared the Narrows an hour later. It was about 7.0 a.m., and light enough to see properly through the periscope and get an accurate fix. He was just below Nagara Point. The Point itself was clearly visible, backed by the earth-works of the fort which covered it on the landward side. But there was no great ship aground in the shallows. The *Goeben* had gone.

After all they had gone through it was a bitter blow. White proceeded further up the Straits until he could see clear water to the east—the long leg which runs to Gallipoli. There was no sign of the battle-cruiser. It was useless to continue. He must turn back empty-handed, very conscious now of the long and dangerous miles which must be covered in broad daylight to regain the open sea. He would have to nurse the battery which, after ten and a half hours dived and their struggles with the obstruction on the way up, was getting low. Grimly he reversed his course.

The Narrows were safely negotiated without any interference from the enemy. With the strong current astern it did not take long, even at low speed. At about 8.45 a.m. E 14 was nearing Chanak. White put up the periscope to check his position and sighted a Turkish ship within easy firing range.

It was a large merchant ship, a Fleet Auxiliary which had been used by the Turks to disembark the *Goeben's* ammunition during the efforts to lighten and refloat her. This White could not know, but she was clearly a worthwhile target. He ordered 'Fifty feet' whilst both bow tubes were made ready. A minute or two later he rose to periscope depth, waited for a short time until the sights came on, and fired. E 14 trembled slightly as first one and then a second torpedo sped towards the target.

Eleven seconds after the order 'Fire Two' there was a tremendous explosion. The cause is still unexplained. E 14 would still have been in the Narrows minefield. Perhaps a torpedo had hit and set off a mine. The explosion was very close at hand and E 14 was violently shaken, lifted bodily for ten or fifteen feet and brought almost to the surface. Her conning tower was now right out of the water and the forts immediately opened fire. The range was short and the Turks saw several unmistakable hits. They had no doubt that they had sunk the intruder when the submarine disappeared.

But E 14 was still alive. White had forced her under again. She was very 'heavy', plunging down and hitting the bottom at 150 feet before control could be regained.

White stopped his motors and called for reports of damage. Most of the lights had been shattered by the shock, and the boat was in half-darkness, lit only by feeble auxiliary lamps. Water could be heard gushing in forward and aft.

But it seemed that things were not as bad as might have been expected. The forehatch and engine-room hatch were sprung and leaking badly, but the pressure hull was intact. All the vital machinery was still apparently in working order. Surface craft could be heard passing overhead and a few depth-charges were dropped, but none fell close. The Turks were pretty certain they had already made a 'kill', though they sent a few patrols down the Straits as a precaution. Gradually the sounds of this hunt died away.

Like a gallant boxer after a punishing round, E 14 was still on her feet but very groggy. The vital battery was low, as were the scarcely less vital supplies of high pressure air for blowing tanks. She was some fifteen miles from safety, with the Kephez minefield to negotiate. Further, as she left the bottom to continue her journey, it was quickly clear that the damage she had suffered was more

1. Lieutenant N. D. Holbrook. V.C.. R.N.

2.   Lieutenant Commander E. C. Boyle, V.C., R.N.

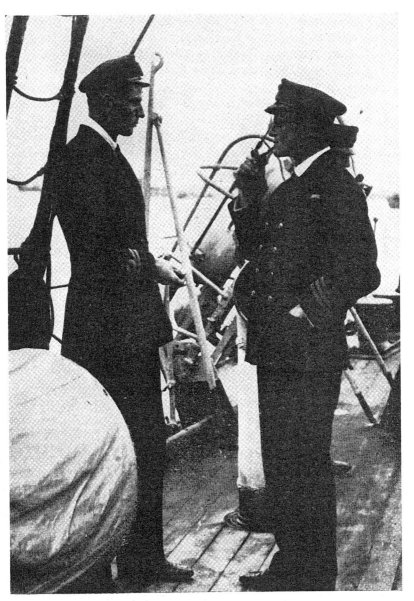

3. Commander M. D. Nasmith, V.C., R.N.
(with Lieutenant G. D'Oyly-Hughes, D.S.O., R.N.)

4. Lieutenant R. D. Sandford, V.C., R.N.

5. Lieutenant Commander G. Saxton White, V.C., R.N.

6. Lieutenant Commander M. D. Wanklyn, V.C., D.S.O., R.N. (centre, with officers and men of H.M. Submarine *Upholder*)

7a. Lieutenant P. S. W. Roberts, V.C., D.S.C., R.N.
(photographed with his wife, after the investiture in
Buckingham Palace)

7b. Petty Officer T. Gould, V.C.
(with Lieutenant H. S. Mackenzie, D.S.O., R.N.)

8. Commander A. C. C. Miers, V.C., D.S.O., R.N.

9. Commander J. W. Linton, V.C., D.S.O., D.S.C., R.N.

10. Lieutenant D. Cameron, V.C., R.N.R.

11.   Lieutenant B. C. G. Place, V.C., D.S.C., R.N.

12b. Leading Seaman J. J. Magennis, V.C.

12a. Lieutenant I. E. Fraser, V.C., D.S.C., R.N.R.

extensive than had been apparent. She was inexplicably 'heavy' and, when a trim had been caught, very difficult to control. Steering and depth-keeping were erratic. It was impossible to maintain a straight course or keep at a steady depth. When, as was essential, White came to periscope depth to get a fix, full speed had to be used to avoid breaking surface.

For something like two hours E 14 struggled on, creeping towards the mouth of the Straits. Near Kephez she passed under the Turkish patrols, returning to Chanak. The coast was now clear, but the battery was almost exhausted.

Water was leaking from the hatches faster than the pumps could take it and rising steadily in the bilges, particularly in the fore end. E 14 began to take on an angle down by the bow, though all the forward auxiliary tanks had been emptied. The loose water gushed forward in an oily torrent, the angle became more extreme, and E 14 plunged to 165 feet before she could be brought up by partially blowing some of the main ballast tanks, using high-pressure air which could ill be spared from the rapidly dwindling supplies. With the boat now almost impossible to control, the battery nearly exhausted and only three partly filled bottles of air remaining, White decided he could no longer struggle on submerged.

At this point most men would have admitted defeat. For 18 hours, almost without a break, White had been dealing with a constant succession of difficulties. He, his crew and his submarine were very near the end of their strength. But White was undaunted. Though still under the guns of the forts on Cape Helles and Kum Kale, the open sea was ahead. He would come up and run the gauntlet. 'Surface,' he ordered, 'stand by both engines.'

With the last of the air the tanks were blown. White stood in the control room watching the diving-gauges swing back. Twenty, fifteen, ten feet. The conning tower would now be clear of the water. 'Open up' he ordered.

But the hatch would not move, for the conning-tower, hit by shell-fire earlier, was full of water.

It could be drained, but this would take several minutes. Until a hatch had been opened the diesel engines could not be started. White ordered the fore-hatch to be used. It was not a quick-opening hatch like the conning-tower and it seemed an age before it was flung back. The Turks had spotted E 14 and opened fire upon her, as she moved slowly on the motors. Shells from the forts on both sides of the Straits were falling near as White at last gained the deck, followed by the navigating officer, Lieutenant Drew R.N.R., and the coxswain.

After the oil-smelling gloom below it seemed a different world. The sun was shining, the sea was blue. White fountains of spray rose on either side as shells cracked into the water. E 14 seemed to be moving very slowly, but soon the diesels rumbled into life. The hull began to vibrate as she forged ahead faster.

A submarine is a small target and for some time she escaped further damage. Had it been possible to steer from the bridge, using the wheel on the top of the conning tower, she might have been able to dodge the shell-fire more effectively, but the shaft passing down below had been severed. Even as it was it was some time before the Turks scored a direct hit. This shell, landing on the bow, did no vital damage; but clearly the end was near. To give his crew some chance of escaping alive White ordered a turn to port towards the shore. Soon afterwards a shell exploded near the conning tower, killing White and Drew. A few minutes later another shell pierced the pressure hull. E 14, still crawling towards the safety she would now never reach, began to sink. Telegraphist Pritchard, who with Signalman Trimbell had been trying to hoist the mast to get off a message asking for assistance, was badly wounded and blown into the sea. Able Seaman Mitchell dived in after him, followed by Trimbell, and succeeded in keeping Pritchard afloat. A few more men joined them in the water as E 14 filled and sank, but the

First Lieutenant, Lieutenant Jack Blissett and twenty-seven ratings were missing. When last seen Blissett was standing in the engine room, directing the men who were still at their posts. So died E 14, one of the most famous ships of World War I.

Not until she had disappeared did the guns cease firing. Later a tug arrived, manned by a mixed Turco-German crew, and picked up the nine survivors. The wounded were taken to hospital, but the others spent the rest of this very long day being interrogated.

Next day the Turkish communiqué announced that they had sunk a submarine. The bitter news was received as an aircraft, returning from a flight over Constantinople, reported that the *Goeben* was lying off the Dockyard in the Golden Horn.

It was months before any further news was received on the Allied side. In May a letter came through from a prison camp in Asia Minor, written by Petty Officer Robert Perkins, the coxswain and senior survivor. It is a remarkable letter, making no mention of his plight, at forced labour in the cement works at Eski Hissar and suffering great privations. Perkins wrote of what had happened on 28 January. In simple words he movingly expresses what he and his shipmates thought of Geoffrey White. He concludes: —

> 'It was a credit to us all to think we had such a brave Captain, and Sir, if only I could mention a few things about him, but owing to his coolness he saved the boat half a dozen times.'

Early in 1919, when the prisoners were repatriated, the story of E 14's last fight was finally told, and on 24 May the London Gazette published the citation in which Lieutenant-Commander Geoffrey Saxton White was posthumously awarded the Victoria Cross.

CHAPTER SEVEN

WANKLYN AND *UPHOLDER*

THE submarines of the earlier chapters of this book were designed and built without the guide of any wartime experience. As was to be expected, development during the 1914-18 war was rapid. Progress continued from 1918 to 1939, and the submarines with which we began the 1939-45 war were a considerable improvement on those which had borne the brunt of the fighting twenty-five years before. The submarine is a weapon of attack and the defence had not been idle. U-boats had come very near to winning World War I for Germany, and the development of anti-submarine measures had been given top priority by the Allies. Other nations had followed suit, and the principle navies of 1939 were well equipped with devices for finding and attacking submarines. Invisibility was still the submarine's chief defence, but the cloak had been partly torn. Anti-submarine vessels could locate a submerged submarine, though luckily for the submarine not with absolute certainty or at long range. Charges set to explode at a pre-determined depth could then be dropped or fired from mortars in a 'pattern' which covered a considerable area and a wide range of depths. Submarines had stronger hulls, and the depth-charges must fall close to do vital damage. Their torpedoes were more powerful, more accurate and could be fired 'blind' at longer range, using the same type of instrument to locate the target as was used by the defence against the submarine. Instruments had also been developed to work out how far ahead of the target torpedoes should be aimed to score a hit—the vital D.A. or direct angle which, early in the 1914-18 war, had been largely a matter of 'eye'.

During an attack the submarine's own courses and speeds, the bearing of the enemy, his approximate range and estimated speed were fed into a form of computer known as the 'fruit machine', which automatically provided a D.A.

But the greatest disability remained—the electric battery of strictly limited capacity on which the submerged submarine still relied. Speed under water was no higher than in the 1914-18 war and much more dangerous to use, because of the sensitive listening devices carried by surface ships. A submerged submarine had a little more latitude now in the depth at which she moved, but was still only able to crawl away at a slow walking pace if she did not wish to tell all the world where she was. True, she could herself listen to and locate her enemies, a big advantage in really skilful hands. She could dodge, though only in slow motion. All in all it might be said that the balance had shifted in favour of the surface ship in areas where the defence was concentrated and well-organised. On the other hand the modern submarine had better sea-keeping qualities and a much longer radius of action. By going farther afield the submarine could operate where patrols were thin on the ground, and here the advantage rested squarely with the submarine, or would have done had it not been for the air.

The greatest change affecting submarine operations in World War II has been left to the last. The submarine of 1939 like the submarine of 1914 was still only a *sub-mersible*—a ship which could hold its breath and dive below the surface of the sea for a limited period. It could only travel from one place to another on the surface; on patrol it must come to the surface daily and for several hours to re-charge its batteries. Huge areas of sea could now be searched by patrolling aircraft; when the water was clear, as in the Mediterranean, they could even spot a submarine at periscope depth. The development of radar, very rapid from 1939 onwards, made it possible for aircraft and surface ships to locate a submarine on the

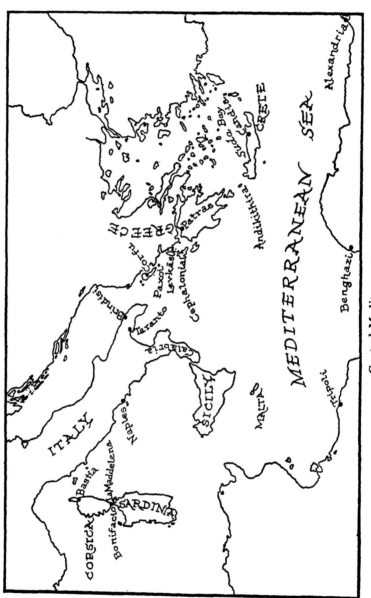

Central Mediterranean

surface at night and in thick weather. The submarine countered this by developing the schnorkel—a breathing tube which enabled it to cruise and charge its batteries at periscope depth, but none of the submarines which feature in this book were equipped with such a device.

1941 was a critical year for the Allies, particularly in the Mediterranean. On land fighting surged to and fro along the North African coast. It was a battle whose outcome depended to a large extent on the supply-lines of the opposing armies. Our army based on Egypt relied on lines stretching for 12,000 miles down the Red Sea, round the Cape and up through the South and North Atlantic. The Axis, based on Tripolitania, had to bring its ammunition, fuel and other supplies across the Mediterranean—only a few hundred miles, but vital nonetheless. For our armies in North Africa the problem could be simply stated. If the Axis could bring in their supplies unhindered, defeat was certain. Everything depended on reducing the traffic from Italian ports, but how could this be done? The Axis supply lines were about 1,000 miles from our fleet bases at Gibraltar and Alexandria, under the umbrella of large numbers of enemy aircraft. Surface forces could not be used effectively. Malta was the key, a fact fully realised by both sides.

Books have been written about the heroic defence of Malta and the costly efforts to keep our only effective forward base supplied. In June 1940 the Malta Submarine Force was formed, an off-shoot of the First Submarine Flotilla in Alexandria, from January 1941 under the command of Commander G. W. G. Simpson. Until the eventual defeat of the Axis in North Africa a handful of small submarines, based on Malta except for one short break, was to play a considerable part in interfering with the Axis supply lines across the Mediterranean, suffering very heavy casualties in the process, but paying an effective dividend. This is the background, necessarily very brief, for the story of Lieutenant Commander M. D. Wanklyn and H.M. Submarine *Upholder*.

Malcolm David Wanklyn was born in London in 1911 and joined the Royal Naval College at Dartmouth before his fourteenth birthday. He was a quiet, clever boy with a taste for science and mathematics. That he had brains was confirmed when he was awarded the maximum number of first class certificates in his courses for Lieutenant six years later. Those with 'five ones' are the Navy's intellectuals, though not always its best officers, but Wanklyn had plenty of character and a strong personality; effective and practical as well as intelligent. He volunteered for submarines in 1933, was married in 1938, was given his first command in 1940 and carried out a number of war patrols in the Channel and North Sea. In the same year he was appointed to a submarine of the 'U' class building at Barrow in Furness. After trials and a short 'working up' period Wanklyn took *Upholder* to the Mediterranean to join the Malta Submarine Force in December.

Upholder was, by the standards of the time, a small submarine, almost exactly the same size as the 'E' boats of the 1914-18 war. She was armed with four 21-inch torpedo tubes, all in the bow, and carried eight torpedoes. A 12-pounder gun was mounted in front of the conning tower. Her maximum speed was 12 knots on the surface and 10 knots submerged. The U class were excellent little submarines, quick-diving, manoeuverable and easy to handle.

The waters in which the Malta submarines operated were confined and dangerous, heavily patrolled by the very considerable Italian Navy operating close to its numerous bases. The *Regia Aeronautica,* as the naval arm of the Italian Air Force was called, had almost undisputed command of the air. The Eastern and Western basins of the Mediterranean are deep, but in the centre between Sicily, the toe and heel of Italy and the N. African coast is a comparatively shallow shelf much of which can be effectively mined. After the strain of a long patrol the submarines had no safe, well-equipped base to which to return. From January 1941 to May 1942 Malta was the target of air attacks whose savage intensity is well known. A scheme to build proper submarine shelters in the easily tunnelled sandstone had been turned down before the war. Now it was too late. Early in 1941 the Luftwaffe was concentrating on the dockyard and the Grand Harbour, but the submarine 'trot' off Manoel Island was close to the target area and maintenance work was hindered by the constant alerts. Food and drink was reasonably plentiful, but the munitions of war, brought to Malta from Gibraltar and Alexandria, were frequently destroyed on the way. Fuel, torpedoes, spare parts and other vital necessities were never more than marginally available. Relaxations were few.

Upholder's first war patrol from Malta was in January 1941. On her second day out she attacked two supply ships, missing both of them and wasting four precious torpedoes. Two days later, when on the surface in the small hours charging her battery, she again sighted two supply ships. Warned by his previous experience Wanklyn closed to 900 yards before firing and was rewarded with a hit. When dawn came the target was still afloat, but under water up to her bridge. Deciding she would sink 'without further assistance' Wanklyn continued his patrol, sighted a small convoy two days later and sank another ship. The escorts counter-attacked with depth charges but *Upholder* got away undamaged. Commander Simpson reported that this first patrol had been well executed.

But the promise of that patrol was not at first fulfilled. Attacks were carried out during *Upholder's* second and third patrols, but no hits were scored. For his fourth patrol he was sent to the waters off Sicily. He returned with useful information about enemy movements, but no other results. Wanklyn, later probably the most famous British submarine commander of the 1939-45 war, was proving a slow starter.

On her fifth patrol, early in April 1941, *Upholder* had three good opportunities, made three attacks, fired a total of eight torpedoes, and missed with them all. Wanklyn was returning to Malta without any real means of offence when he sighted an escorted convoy in the darkness shortly before dawn. Approaching on the surface he ordered gun action stations, had *Upholder's* little 12 pounder loaded with starshell and fired into the sky ahead of the enemy ships. The convoy, thinking that an attack by surface forces must be imminent, turned back on its tracks. Wanklyn remained on the surface and signalled an enemy report before being put down by the escorting destroyers. The signal had not been acknowledged. Daylight had now come, but he surfaced again, in the full view of four aircraft which had now appeared, and signalled an amplifying report.

The patrol reports of Malta Force Submarines were passed through the parent flotilla. Wanklyn's non-success in four successive patrols, culminating in the missed opportunities of the last few days, were raising doubts about his competence. Torpedoes were in such short supply that they had to be taken from a submarine returning from patrol to try and complete the outfit of one going out. A Commanding Officer who recorded too many 'misses' was a serious liability to the whole flotilla. The covering remarks, forwarding the report on *Upholder's* fifth patrol to the Admiralty, praised his actions in turning back the convoy, but contained some acid comments on the failures to hit with his torpedoes. Even Simpson, with whom he had served in a submarine before the war and who had a very high opinion of his capabilities, was beginning to wonder if that very promising first patrol had been a flash in the pan. It was the nadir of Wanklyn's fortunes, but also the turning-point of his career.

The doubts were not shared by *Upholder's* crew. Even in those early days, before he had made his reputation, Wanklyn had that extra something, impossible to describe, which makes some men command a sort of unspoken reverence from their fellows and inspire them with the wish to please. The quiet little boy had grown into a quiet young man, friendly, but always a little formidable. He was extremely thorough, a perfectionist, but not a fusser. The 'skipper' insisted on the highest standards, but was just and patient with those genuinely doing their best. At sea he had their complete confidence, an all-important factor for the lives of his three officers and thirty-four ratings were often completely in his hands. Morale was high in *Upholder* when she sailed on her sixth patrol on 21 April.

Three days later Wanklyn sighted a convoy. Determined not to miss again he closed to 700 yards and sank the *Antonietta Laura* of 5,428 tons. His next assignment was a tricky one. An Italian destroyer and a German merchant ship had been abandoned on a shoal after an attack on a convoy by surface ships. *Upholder* was told to try and finish them off. A submarine in shallow water is, of course, highly vulnerable, and *Upholder* went aground when trying to approach the destroyer. Baulked, but not frustrated, Wanklyn made his way alongside the merchant ship, searched her thoroughly and set her on fire. It was broad daylight and *Upholder* would be quite unable to dive if enemy aircraft or surface ships appeared, but Wanklyn withdrew successfully. A few days later he sighted a convoy of five merchant ships escorted by no less than four destroyers. The sea was rough with a heavy swell which made depth-keeping difficult, but he brought *Upholder* in unobserved, fired a salvo of four torpedoes and scored three hits, sinking one ship and heavily damaging another. Under heavy counter-attack by the destroyers Wanklyn withdrew, re-loaded his tubes with the two torpedoes remaining, closed and sank the damaged ship and returned to Malta. This was the true Wanklyn touch, henceforth to be repeated again and again.

Simpson was delighted. After a fortnight in harbour for maintenance and rest, he sent them off again. At first it seemed that the jinx of the early patrols had returned. One of the torpedoes already loaded in its tube developed a leak and had to be changed—a tricky operation when none had been fired and the fore-end was encumbered by the four spares. Three days later the asdic set went out of action. This was a most serious matter, robbing *Upholder* of her ability to 'listen' for approaching enemy ships or to pick up the searching impulses of destroyers— an invaluable help in avoiding counter-attacks. Wanklyn was 'deaf' when he sighted a convoy on the following day.

The conditions for a successful attack were exceedingly difficult, with the enemy ships, steaming close inshore, almost invisible against the land. Without an asdic set to help him Wanklyn pressed home his attack, fired three torpedoes and scored a hit. The following day he attacked another heavily escorted convoy and again scored a hit. A heavy counter-attack followed which continued all the afternoon, but Wanklyn, evading the enemy by inspired guess-work, got away without damage.

Many men might now rightly have considered that providence had been tempted far enough. The asdic set was still out of action, only two torpedoes remained; the bow-cap of one of the loaded tubes was difficult to operate and the patrol was almost at an end. Wanklyn ordered the torpedo to be re-loaded in another tube, and remained on his billet.

On the evening of 24 May *Upholder* was at periscope depth, keeping a sharp lookout. It was the close of a stormy day, with a rough sea. At 8.30 p.m. the sun had just set, but the western sky was still an angry red. Sunset and dawn are bad times for a submarine, not light enough for much to be seen through the periscope and too light for surface operations. It was in this half-light that a convoy appeared; three very large ships steaming fast with several destroyers in company.

The height of the swell, with the tops of the waves washing right over the periscope, and the gathering dusk made observation difficult. As the dark water fell away Wanklyn could distinguish the silhouettes of three large, two-funnelled ships against the afterglow, but the smaller destroyers, disposed around them, were almost invisible. Without listening gear he could only estimate the convoy's speed, but it was certainly high. He could not count the destroyers, or see just where they were, but this was clearly a troop convoy and would be strongly escorted. On the other hand he was in a good position, ahead and not far off its track. A long range shot would be comparatively safe, but with only two torpedoes probably unfruitful. There was only one place to fire to ensure success—right amongst the destroyers which he could neither see nor hear. The convoy was zig-zagging, and now it altered course towards *Upholder,* rapidly shortening the range.

This was the sort of occasion where Wanklyn was always to show his brilliance. He was a rapid thinker with a very clear mind. Ordering the two tubes to be brought to the ready Wanklyn estimated the big ships' speed at 20 knots, aimed at the centre of the three and fired. As he gave the order he saw a destroyer close ahead. He had no time to locate the others before going deep. *Upholder* had levelled off at 150 feet when her crew heard the thump of an explosion, followed almost immediately by a second thump. Two hits! Splendid, but now for the inevitable retribution. At dead slow speed to avoid helping the enemy *Upholder* waited, listening. The defective asdic set would have given some indication of what the destroyers were doing and which way to turn to get away. As it was Wanklyn, completely blind and completely deaf, was like a man surrounded by enemies in a pitch-black room. He could only guess what he ought to do.

That the destroyers would locate *Upholder* was a certainty, a certainty that was soon confirmed. Two minutes after the torpedoes had left the tubes the counter-attack began. At first the depth-charges were not very close. *Upholder,* with every unnecessary motor stopped, crept along, hoping the destroyers would fail to get an accurate fix of her position. Her crew sat or stood at their posts; silent, straining their ears for sounds from above.

The pause, and it could be nothing more, was almost unbearably prolonged.

At such moments the captain of a submarine with the whole weight of decision on his shoulders must also possess, and give out, the moral strength which will uphold his crew. The weaker men, of whom there must be one or two, will be very near breaking point. Covertly they watch the only person who knows what has happened and what is likely to befall. Great commanders, like David Wanklyn, exude confidence—a confidence they may be very far from feeling themselves.

It was almost a relief when the destroyers could be heard again. Two of them seemed to be working together. Charges began to fall closer. Each explosion was like a great hammer hitting the hull. *Upholder* twisted and turned and altered her depth as Wanklyn, unflurried and quiet spoken, tried to guess the enemy's tactics. Four charges crashed off very close, the shock waves shaking *Upholder* violently. Lights broke; things smashed to the deck; cork from the finish inside the hull rained down. A destroyer rumbled overhead, her propeller beats only too clearly audible without the assistance of any listening apparatus. If she dropped a pattern now it would probably be the last one they would ever hear; a shattering impact followed by the terrible sound of water gushing in through the damaged hull. In the control room men looked at Wanklyn, but he seemed quite relaxed. Stilling their fears they waited for the next convulsion.

Miraculously it never came. The hunt moved away. For nearly a quarter of an hour there was silence. Hopes were rising when another sound broke the stillness. Light taps, like searching fingers, scratching at *Upholder's* hull. What was it? A sweep wire? The taps continued for ten minutes. Wanklyn, rightly decided that it was a sinking ship breaking up as she plunged to the bottom, flexed his big, expressive hands. 'Time for a mug of tea' he said. Everybody grinned. It was the accepted signal that the counter-attack was over. At 10.50 p.m. he cautiously brought *Upholder* to the surface. She was still quite close to the scene of the attack. The heaving sea was empty, but there was a strong smell of oil fuel.

Upholder had sunk the *Conte Rosso,* 18,000 tons and crammed with troops. The rest of the convoy had turned back.

This was the patrol for which Wanklyn was awarded the Victoria Cross some months later, but there was now no doubt that 'Wanks' was a submarine commander of quite exceptional merit. Many have some of the qualities needed, but it is rare to find them all in one man. He was fearless, but not reckless. In the tightest corners he was unflurried, calm, concise in his orders. He took great risks, but they were calculated risks, in which the chances were quickly and accurately assessed and accepted when there was a proper, if very narrow, margin in his favour. The movements of his own submarine, of the target he was attacking and of the escorts were parts of an intricate problem whose solution remained always within his grasp. A brilliant applied mathematician, but a very human man, always aware that success could only be achieved and disaster averted if *Upholder's* officers and men did a little better than might be expected and were a little less fallible than could be feared. His crew responded by becoming a cut above the average. Bad hats drafted to *Upholder* no longer appeared at the defaulters' table. They soon fell under the spell of this tall, un-selfconscious, distinguished-looking man with the sort of eyes which you did not forget.

Wanklyn, doing his job with a sort of dedicated concentration, had a 'fire in his belly', but there was another side to his character only seen by his closest friends. The thought of killing other men, men with wives and children, young men with their lives before them, was abhorrent to him. He recognised that it had to be done, but he hated doing it. The feeling of triumph in mastering a difficult and dangerous problem was short lived. Afterwards would come what another very brave fighter (David

Beatty) had called the 'everlasting, bitter regrets'. This most formidable of submarine commanders was, at heart, a very gentle man.

All through the summer of 1941 *Upholder* continued to add to her bag, and to escape damage. The risks were very real. From a flotilla, (Simpson's Malta Submarines became the 10th Submarine Flotilla in September), never stronger than ten submarines, *Usk* was sunk in April, *Undaunted* in May, *Union* in July, P 32 and P 33 in August. It was a very trying life. Patrols, during which danger was never absent, lasted about twelve days. The enemy had command of the air and should have dominated the surface of the sea. Large areas of the Central Mediterranean were heavily mined and new fields were always being laid. Well-armed, fast motor boats, very difficult to see, were a constant menace when charging the battery on the surface at night. Attacks on convoys would be followed by counter-attacks by the escorts as surely as night follows day. Malta had serious limitations as a base. Enemy air attacks were less intense from July to December, but it was still a beleaguered fortress, short of many of the essentials of war and of ordinary life. Everything possible was done to give the submarine crews, who virtually never saw the daylight on patrol, rest and relaxation in harbour, but facilities were limited. The crews themselves were very young, with a sprinkling of more experienced men, and these older men had sometimes to be taken away to give a backbone to newly commissioned submarines. Green men, without patrol experience, were a liability until they had proved themselves, and not every man could measure up to what was demanded of him, though failures were exceedingly rare. The strain on commanding officers was tremendous. From the moment their submarines left Malta they were constantly on call day and night. Decisions vital to the safety of the boat and crew were continually required of them. When opportunities occurred success depended almost entirely on their judgement. Under depth-charge attack it was often their skill and theirs alone which averted disaster.

By mid-September *Upholder* had carried out thirteen patrols, the majority of which had been successful. She had sunk a number of ships, and damaged many others. (Once she scored two hits on a cruiser steaming at 28 knots—an astonishing feat.) Skill in attack was matched by skill in defence. Thirty-eight depth charges followed the torpedoing of the cruiser; forty-eight in eight minutes the sinking of a tanker; thirty-three after an attempt to intercept some troopships on a day of glassy calm. In none of these attacks had *Upholder* suffered any serious damage.

With improved Intelligence it was now sometimes possible to anticipate important enemy movements, and on 17 September she was one of four submarines sent to try to intercept a convoy for Tripoli. At 1.30 a.m. she was patrolling on the surface when her gyro compass failed, leaving her with only a somewhat erratic magnetic compass to steer by. *Unbeaten* sighted the convoy, too far off for an attack, but signalled their position and approximate course and speed. *Upholder* saw the darkened ships at 3.40 a.m. and closed on the surface at full speed. Three very large ships with an escort of four or more destroyers loomed up, steaming fast—a troop convoy. Wanklyn decided to remain on the surface. He was in a good position on the convoy's bow, but the swinging compass card of the small magnetic compass made it impossible for the helmsman to hold a very straight course. In the swell which was running *Upholder* yawed from side to side as she closed the range. All four bow tubes were brought to the ready. On the swaying bridge Wanklyn watched the great ships loom closer through his night-glasses. The destroyers screening them were difficult to see, but they had not spotted *Upholder* when Wanklyn fired a full salvo of four torpedoes. It was a difficult shot. An error of one or two degrees would mean missing instead of hitting and the yaw prevented him steadying *Upholder* on an exact bearing. He had to judge the swing of the bow between the order to fire each torpedo and the moment it actually left the tube. The salvo must be 'spread', like a slightly opened fan, to cover a bigger area and give the best chance of hitting. Off went the first two torpedoes at short intervals as *Upholder* yawed to starboard; two more followed them as she swung back to port. Wanklyn, who had already sent the look-outs below, clambered down the conning tower, pressed the diving klaxon and pulled the hatch shut behind him.

Upholder levelled off below the surface. Everyone strained their ears, waiting. Four minutes after firing there was the sound of an explosion, followed a little later by another. At least two hits. (As a matter of fact there had been three.) *Upholder* went deep and waited for the expected counter-attack, but the Italian destroyers were so busy standing by the damaged troopships that it never came. The *Netunia* had gone to the bottom, the *Oceania* was gravely stricken and the *Oriana* had made off at full speed. All were ships of about 19,000 tons, packed with troops.

Three quarters of an hour later Wanklyn came to the surface. It was still dark, but he distinguished one large ship, stopped, but still afloat with a couple of destroyers in attendance. *Upholder* went deep whilst she reloaded her tubes, steering east to be up-sun at dawn. At daylight, with four torpedoes ready, Wanklyn again closed the stopped ship. He was just about to fire when he spotted the stem of a destroyer, bearing down on *Upholder,* and had to go deep in a hurry. This put him in the wrong position for the coup-de-grace, so he continued under the destroyer and the *Oceania* and came to periscope depth on the other side.

'Fire One'; a few seconds later, 'Fire Two'. Both torpedoes hit and the liner turned over and sank in eight minutes. *Unbeaten,* who had approached during the night and was also about to fire, was surprised to see her target list and disappear.

This was *Upholder*'s fourteenth patrol. For the rest

of the year her successes continued—many supply ships, two destroyers. The nineteenth patrol, just before Christmas, was a blank, so unusual an event for Wanklyn that the covering remarks from his Admiral forwarding the report to the Admiralty contained a comment to this effect.

The successes of the little submarines of the Tenth Flotilla had the enemy seriously worried. In September 1941 the German Staff in Italy, referring to the armies in N. Africa, reported that 'a very severe supply crisis must occur relatively soon'. In mid-November Hitler personally approved sending German technicians with anti-submarine material and devices to the Mediterranean. In December the Luftwaffe re-appeared over Malta. Heavy daylight raids began, first on the dockyard and airfields, but soon seeking out the submarine base and the submarines themselves for sustained and violent attention. Fighters beat up submarines entering and leaving harbour with cannon fire; they had to remain submerged to the last minute, or enter and leave in the dark. Even in harbour there was no safety, accurate day-bombing forcing the submarines to submerge from sunrise to sunset. For men returning from an arduous patrol it was a heavy additional strain. Simpson could not provide reliefs for all the crew, half of which now spent their 'rest' period sitting on the bottom of the harbour during the day, doing the maintenance work which had accumulated at sea by night. Of course the work was dislocated, and the bigger jobs needing Dockyard help meant exposing the submarines to great risks. P 31 was damaged beyond repair whilst in dock during the raids of 6 January, and worse was to follow.

Of the ten boats which had formed the Malta flotilla a year earlier only *Upholder, Urge* and *Unbeaten* remained. Three had been sunk on patrol; four had left Malta to be refitted or repaired. Some of the blanks had been filled by new arrivals, though it was the proven crews of long experience which were naturally the most valuable. But there was a limit to the times the pitcher could be sent to the well, and fifteen patrols was about as much as most commanding officers, on whom the heaviest burden was placed, could stand before being given a long rest in really peaceful surroundings. Wanklyn had done nineteen patrols at the turn of the year, but had so far successfully pleaded his case to be allowed to remain. 'Shrimp' Simpson, now a Captain, kept a very close eye on all his submarine crews. David Wanklyn was a close personal friend as well as his best C.O. Outwardly Wanklyn was still the same calm, unflurried figure. Perhaps the fire within burnt a little nearer the surface, but his efficiency was unimpaired and *Upholder* continued to add to her successes.

January was a month of almost continuous daylight alerts. Heavy attacks partially destroyed the submarine base. The rest camps at the other end of the island were machine-gunned and bombed. Even on the bottom of the harbour safety was only comparative, for the enemy began methodically to plaster the deep water anchorages, as well as attacking every submarine in sight. *Upright, Una, P 30* and *P 39* were damaged, two of them beyond repair. The Polish *Sokol* was hit on a number of occasions and the Greek *Glavkos* sunk. *Pandora,* bringing stores to Malta was destroyed as she was unloading. *P 38* was lost on patrol. Sea or harbour there was no respite, little rest and no real safety. And now the small flotilla of minesweepers which swept the approaches to Malta suffered severe losses. Soon only one remained effective, and a clear channel could not be guaranteed. Simpson began to wonder how long his flotilla could survive. Damage to the submarines apart, the crews must have proper rest between patrols. The strain, particularly on those who had already had many months of arduous duty, was almost intolerable.

Wanklyn was looking tired, but his professional brilliance was unblunted. In January, returning from patrol with only two torpedoes left, he encountered the Italian submarine *Ammiraglio St. Bon* in the moonlight. Both submarines were on the surface. The Italian opened fire with her gun. Instead of replying in kind Wanklyn dived, knowing that the enemy could not get under quickly with her guns' crew on deck and guessing his opponent would alter course away as soon as he lost his target, an accurate appreciation. *Upholder's* first torpedo missed but her second, and last, hit below the conning tower, putting paid to the *St. Bon*.

Because of an important Alexandria to Malta convoy for which submarine cover was ordered *Upholder* had only six days in harbour after this patrol. Wanklyn, like other very sensitive men, had considerable reserves of nervous energy, but Simpson insisted on him having a short break, arranging for another C.O., Lieutenant Norman, to take *Upholder* on her twenty-second patrol early in February. Wanklyn went off to the camp at Ghain Tuffeiha to rest in the winter sunshine. It was a pity he could not indulge in his favourite hobby of dry-fly fishing for trout, but he had his collection of stamps (he was an expert philatelist) to study and enjoy. He was relaxed and refreshed when he went off again from 21 February to 5 March, sinking an escorted supply ship in his usual polished manner, with two hits out of three torpedoes fired. But Simpson had already decided that Wanklyn must have a real rest very soon. *Upholder* was due for docking and refit in England in April, after her twenty-fifth patrol. Wanklyn suggested that he should take over another submarine and remain in Malta to 'add to his bag', but Simpson was adamant; he must go home in his ship.

During the past fourteen months the two men had become very close. Wanklyn's departure would leave a gap, both on and off duty, which could not be filled, and Simpson would miss his friend's support and wise counsel. But this was not a personal matter; men like Wanklyn were a national asset. The whole island would be sorry when he left, for *Upholder* had become a symbol in that hard-pressed place, which spent its days taking dreadful punishment with very little chance of striking back. The lanky, modest figure with blazing eyes and ragged beard and his super-efficient crew were a spear in the enemy's side.

On 14 March *Upholder* left for her twenty-fourth patrol, slipping out of harbour at dusk. Four days later she was diving off Brindisi. Wanklyn noticed that ships entering or leaving the harbour were not following a swept channel. With nothing to fear from mines he came close in. Several small vessels came by, none worth a torpedo. Then a U-boat appeared. Wanklyn stalked her, and scored two hits, blowing her to pieces.* Next day he sank a trawler by gunfire before proceeding to the Gulf of Taranto, to take up his position in the line of submarines set across the approaches to the big Italian base during the passage of a Malta convoy.

For three days the submarines waited. March was going out like a lion, with a gale raising a high sea. Clouds raced by close overhead and mist shrouded the horizon. *Upholder*, pumping up and down at periscope depth, was difficult to control. Conditions were almost impossible for a small submarine when the propeller beats of an approaching ship were picked up. Eventually Wanklyn got a glimpse of her above the tumbling, foam-streaked waves. Three dark smudges in the murk; the towering bridge structure and great funnels of a battleship. A full salvo was fired from about 4000 yards, but Wanklyn's luck was out. The battleship, zig-zagging at high speed, altered course after the torpedoes had left the tubes, and all of them missed. Wanklyn was back at Malta on 26 March, and went off to Ghain Tuffeiha with most of his crew for the full rest period of ten days whilst the maintenance men got busy. He was in excellent form when *Upholder* sailed for her twenty-fifth patrol on 6 April.

Her first assignment was to land some agents on the African coast. On the night of 11 April, with this mission

* It was the Italian submarine *Tricheco*.

successfully accomplished, *Upholder* transferred the officer in charge to *Unbeaten* and left for her patrol position off Tripoli. Simpson had learnt that two large merchant ships were preparing to sail and ordered *Upholder, Urge* and *Thrasher* to form a line to intercept them. *Urge* and *Thrasher* took up their stations, but there was no signal from *Upholder*. What had happened? On 14 April *Urge* heard depth-charging which seemed to come from the area where Wanklyn should have been. There was no more news that day, or on the days which followed. It was the sort of blow which shock prevents you at first from feeling. It could not be true! For sixteen long months *Upholder* had never failed eventually to reappear. Four days later the Italians announced that they had sunk a submarine.

Wanklyn had gone.

This was no ordinary loss, and for several weeks an official announcement was withheld, though Mrs. Wanklyn and other relatives were informed. Eventually the Admiralty took the very unusual step of publishing a special communiqué.

'It is seldom proper for Their Lordships to draw distinctions between different services rendered in the course of naval duty, but they take this opportunity of singling out those of H.M.S. *Upholder,* under the command of Lieutenant Commander Wanklyn, for special mention. She was long employed against enemy communications in the Central Mediterranean, and she became noted for the uniformly high quality of her services in that arduous and dangerous duty. Such was the standard of skill and daring, that the ship and her officers and men became an inspiration not only to their own flotilla but to the fleet of which it was a part, and Malta, where for so long H.M.S. *Upholder* was based. The ship and her company are gone, but the example and the inspiration remain.'

CHAPTER EIGHT

ROBERTS AND GOULD

H.M.S. *Thrasher*, of the First Submarine Flotilla, cast off from the depot ship *Medway*, started her diesel engines and turned towards the gate in the boom protecting Alexandria harbour. Outside she dived to adjust her trim, surfaced and set a course for the islands south and east of Greece where she had been ordered to carry out her eighth Mediterranean war patrol. It was the thirteenth of February and a Friday, a fact which had not passed unnoticed by the more superstitious members of her crew of five officers and fifty-one ratings.

Thrasher had returned from a rather disappointing patrol lasting twenty days at the end of January. The weather had been bad and targets few and far between. She had spent several days in the Gulf of Taranto, one of a patrol line of three submarines trying to intercept an Italian force which included a battleship, but it had been blowing a southerly gale, visibility had been bad, and she had seen and heard nothing. Later she had scored her only success, sinking an escorted merchant ship and getting away undamaged from the usual counter-attack. The rest of the patrol had been strenuous, but uneventful.

The 'T' or *Triton* class submarines had been coming into service just before the war. Except for a few special minelayers they were the largest submarines being built for the Royal Navy. After the 1914-18 war, submarines had tended to become a good deal bigger, vessels displacing over 2000 tons submerged, against the 795 tons of the 'E' class. These big ocean-going submarines had good surface characteristics and a very high endurance. Submerged they were less manoeuvrable than smaller boats and much easier for anti-submarine vessels to locate, a fact which was tragically proved by heavy losses in the Mediterranean in 1940-41. In the 'T' class this tendency for increased size had been reversed. They were 269 feet long ('E' class 178 feet; 'U' class 191 feet) and displaced 1575 tons submerged; but they handled well, could dive to 300-350 feet and were popular with their crews. They were very heavily armed, with six internal torpedo tubes in the bow and three external tubes, two in the bow and one in the stern. Later 'T' boats, of which *Thrasher* was one, had two additional external tubes pointing aft. The external tubes were 'one-shot' and could only be re-loaded in harbour, but spares were carried for the six internal tubes so they went to sea with no less than seventeen 21-inch torpedoes. A 4-inch gun, a really useful weapon, was mounted on the casing in front of the conning tower.

Thrasher continued on her way, diving from dawn to dusk to avoid the attentions and unwelcome sighting reports of aircraft, and running on her diesel engines through the night. On 16 February she was approaching her patrol area off Crete. Soon after 4.0 a.m. she sighted a small convoy of three ships, steaming without lights. Lieutenant H. S. Mackenzie, the captain, started his attack, but it was a dark night and the ships were very difficult to see. His estimate of the course the convoy was steering proved to be wrong and the enemy got away, slipping into Candia harbour before he could close the range. After this disappointment *Thrasher* proceeded at full speed towards Suda Bay, diving just before dawn. She was pretty certain she had not been seen.

The sun came up into a clear and cloudless sky. To the south the mountains of Crete, brilliantly capped with snow, stood up out of the calm blue sea, serene and beautiful. Perfect holiday weather, but the worst possible conditions for a submarine. Even at dead slow speed *Thrasher*'s periscope left a long 'V' of ripples on the glassy surface. In the clear waters of the Mediterranean an aircraft would be able to pick out the dark shape of a submarine diving at periscope depth from quite a long way off. If *Thrasher* managed to approach a target unobserved the tracks of her torpedoes would give ample warning to the victim, which could alter course and dodge them. Holiday weather, but certainly not submarine weather. The only favourable factor was the clear sky, giving no cloud-cover to hostile aircraft.

Thrasher began to patrol, remaining at periscope depth and frequently scanning the bright blue dome overhead through the sky-searching window on her high-power periscope, and the unruffled, azure sea.

Lieutenant Mackenzie, the 'old man' of *Thrasher*'s officers, was twenty-seven. A few of the senior ratings were around thirty years of age, but most of the crew were young men. Though young they were experienced, knowing their boat and their jobs and confident in their own ability. All they needed was a chance to get at the enemy, but since the beginning of the year opportunities had been few. When targets are scarce, patrols lasting three weeks, during which daylight is only seen by the officer at the periscope, seem long indeed.

At 8.55 a.m. a small merchant ship appeared. She was not worth a torpedo; gun-action would advertise *Thrasher*'s presence and drive other targets away, so Mackenzie let her go. Fifty minutes later a small patrol craft was sighted in the entrance to Suda Bay. This might mean a convoy so *Thrasher* kept a careful eye upon her. At 10.20 a.m. a motor launch left the harbour, came within a couple of miles of *Thrasher*, patrolled to and fro for a while, and then made off. Through *Thrasher*'s periscope, thrusting up and questing round, it was an aggravatingly peaceful scene. But just before 11 a.m. there was a change.

A Motor Anti-Submarine Launch came tearing out of Suda Bay, throwing up two great bow waves. There were no aircraft in sight so *Thrasher* remained at periscope depth, carefully watching the approaching M.A.S. Mackenzie knew she could not use her submarine detecting gear whilst she was moving fast, but when she stopped

3000 yards off he went deep and turned away to the westward at slow speed. Twenty-five minutes later he came up to see what was happening. The M.A.S. was now some miles away, still stopped and apparently in the same position as before. Clearly she was listening for sub-marines, but had not detected *Thrasher* as she stole quietly away.

It was now 11.20 a.m. The weather was as before, with a cloudless sky and not a ripple on the surface of the sea. Seven miles off, Cape Drepano basked in the sunshine. But against the land was a little cloud of smoke above which Mackenzie spotted an aircraft. Was this a convoy?

For half an hour *Thrasher* waited, moving slowly towards the smoke and keeping a very sharp eye on the aircraft circling above it. A large two-masted schooner skirted the distant coast and turned into Suda Bay. Gradually the masts and single funnel of a medium-sized merchant ship came up over the limited horizon (the top of the periscope was never raised more than a couple of feet above the surface), followed by the upper works and hull. A ship of about 3000 tons, apparently steaming at about 8 knots and deeply laden.

She was not alone. With her was an escort of no less than five anti-submarine vessels, one ahead of her, one on each beam and one on either quarter. The aircraft patrolling overhead appeared to have been joined by another, but of this Mackenzie, taking quick looks through his periscope which he dared not keep up for more than a few seconds at a time, could not be sure. As a precaution he went deep between looks, to eighty feet whilst the target was some distance off and to fifty feet as *Thrasher* drew nearer. It was the sort of weather when he would have preferred to stay deep all the time, using his own listening gear to stalk the enemy, but the propeller beats of the merchant ship were covered and confused by those of her five escorts.

Half an hour after starting her attack *Thrasher* had crept within range. The tubes were at the ready. The escorting A.S. vessels were now very close, but they had not detected her. Raising his periscope to fire, Mackenzie found one of them almost on top of him, and had to go deep to avoid being rammed, missing his chance. When he came up again he was well abaft the merchant ship's beam—not a good position for a shot for she would surely see the approaching torpedoes, turn away and 'comb' their tracks.

But it was now or never. A hit was still possible, though as Mackenzie reported later, 'rather a forlorn hope'.

Thrasher had gone to diving stations at 7.15 a.m. Half an hour later, when Mackenzie was satisfied with the trim and other tests, 'Watch Diving Stations' was ordered. Two-thirds of the crew went to breakfast. At 8 a.m. the watch on duty was relieved and by 9.0 a.m. everyone except the watch was well-fed and fast asleep. There is something about the atmosphere in a submarine which gives men an almost unlimited capacity for eating and sleeping. It was quiet and peaceful as *Thrasher* dived along. Only in the control room was there any sign of activity. The helmsman and the men on the forward and after hydroplanes occasionally moved the wheels which kept *Thrasher* on her course and level at periscope depth. The periscope hissed up and down as the officer on watch raised it above the surface for a look round the horizon and to search the sky overhead. Very occasionally he would order the ballast pump to be started or a flooding valve to be opened to make a small adjustment to the trim.

The sighting of the small merchant ship just before 9.0 a.m. and the patrol craft forty-five minutes later had scarcely interrupted the familiar routine. In both cases Mackenzie was at once informed, came quickly to the control room from the wardroom nearby, had a good look through the periscope and decided to take no action. But he remained awake, and when the motor launch approached at 10.20 stayed in the control room. At 10.0

a.m. the watch was relieved. At 11.0 a.m. came the big moment of the day, when the regulation tot of rum was issued. Half an hour later the watch who would take over at noon sat down to their dinners. They were just finishing them when the sighting of the merchant ship made Mackenzie decide to start an attack. 'Diving Stations!' sent the whole crew scurrying to their posts.

For the next half hour those outside the control room could only deduce what was happening. Right aft, on the stokers' mess deck, the men on duty watched the movements of the after hydroplanes and steering gear. As *Thrasher* went deep, between her peeps at the target, the rudder would move to correct the course, the after hydroplanes go to 'dive' and the depth gauge needle swing round. As the intervals between 'looks' were reduced experience told them that *Thrasher* was closing her target. Would they get near enough to fire? Not much was said, but a feeling of excitement grew. It was not unmixed with carefully hidden trepidation, for attacks were usually followed by a rain of depth-charges.

At the other end of the submarine, in the torpedo compartment, men were busy. Compressed air hissed as the tubes were flooded by blowing water from the tanks immediately below. The bow caps were opened. A small electric telegraph winked, telling the control room that the tubes were now ready.

Thrasher had been at fifty feet. Now she glided up until the big gauges facing coxswain and second coxswain, who controlled the hydroplanes, showed 32 feet. Mackenzie motioned with his hand and the attack periscope came hissing up out of its well. Directly the eyepiece was above the deck he crouched, snapped down the training handles and looked. Nothing but blue water. The periscope crept up. Now a beam of dancing sunlight shone for an instant on the captain's face. Mackenzie motioned the periscope a little higher, swung it quickly round the horizon and stopped on the target. A watching rating quietly reported the bearing to the officer working the 'Fruit machine'. A sign, and the periscope hissed back into its well. A few seconds later it was raised again, this time set to the bearing on which Mackenzie had decided to fire. There was a short pause as the target swam across the field of view. 'Fire one!'

Thrasher trembled slightly as she spat out the first 'fish' of the salvo. The air from the tube, vented inboard to prevent the bubble from rising to the surface and dis-closing her position, gushed into the submarine. Feeling the rise of pressure everyone knew that the torpedo had gone. Three more torpedoes, fired at pre-determined intervals of a few seconds, would now be sent on their way to give the necessary 'spread' and increase the chances of a hit, but before the second one had gone there was a dull, muffled explosion, followed almost immediately by another. The explosions were very close indeed. *Thrasher* trembled and shook as though she had bumped a sub-merged obstruction. What had happened? The last of the salvo had just been fired when there was a pattering noise, like hail on a roof. As Mackenzie gave the order to go deep he guessed the cause of the strange upheaval. An aircraft had dropped a stick of bombs very close to *Thrasher* and sprayed the water above her with machine-gun fire as it zoomed away.

Fortunately there was no apparent damage. *Thrasher* levelled off in the depths and turned away. With water-tight doors between the compartments closed and shallow diving gauges shut off she waited for the next regular item on the programme, the counter-attack. Before it came there was the sound of a loud explosion followed ten seconds later by another. Two of the torpedoes had evidently gone home.

This was highly satisfactory, but *Thrasher* was by no means out of the wood. Her own asdic set told her that three of the anti-submarine vessels up above were in contact. They were still some distance off, but coming closer. The depth-charges began to fall; a series of eleven explosions, each one sounding louder than its predecessor.

A few minutes later ten charges, which seemed to have been dropped more or less together, but spread over a fairly wide area, shook *Thrasher* severely. A short pause and seven more charges crashed off. Some of these were very close indeed. Lights shattered; cork rained down from inside the hull. Men clung for support as the submarine lurched and plunged.

Altogether thirty-three charges were recorded, 'the majority too close to be pleasant'. But now the enemy seemed to lose contact. In the sudden blessed silence *Thrasher* crept away. An hour and a half later she rose cautiously to periscope depth. Three of her tormentors were still hunting in the neighbourhood where she had been so savagely attacked. Beyond them was a very welcome sight; a great column of yellowish-grey smoke from a burning, sinking ship. *Thrasher* went deep to re-load her tubes. When she came to periscope depth again at 3.45 p.m. there was nothing in sight.

For the rest of the day she was undisturbed. The sun set in a blaze of glory. When darkness had fallen Mackenzie came to the surface, intending to move to a new patrol position during the night. It had been a full day, starting with the abortive attack at 4.0 a.m. and including two very narrow escapes, from the bombs of the aircraft and the A.S. vessels. In both cases the margin had been uncommonly narrow. The diesel engines were started, drawing a rush of cool, fresh, night air down the conning tower hatch. Cigarettes and pipes were lit. Tension was relaxed. Men laughed as they moved about below or sat eating supper. But on the bridge the look-outs were vigilant. *Thrasher's* presence would have alerted all patrols. In the darkness small anti-submarine vessels were difficult to see and could get very close unobserved. Everything was ready for an emergency dive, with watch-keepers on the main vent panel and the hydroplanes. The blare of the klaxon would start a routine—ballast tanks flooding, engines stopped and de-clutched, main motors running 'half-ahead', hydroplanes hard to dive—which would have *Thrasher* thirty feet below the surface in less than a minute as the men on the bridge tumbled below. In heavily patrolled enemy waters such emergencies were a common occurrence.

Soon after midnight *Thrasher* passed through the Andikithira channel, leaving Crete on her port quarter. It was a calm, still night, but with hundreds of miles of open sea now ahead she met a long swell from the west. She ploughed slowly along, climbing the oily hills and slipping down into the gentle hollows between them. At 1.30 a.m. she altered course, bringing the swell abeam. *Thrasher* began to roll.

Petty Officer Thomas Gould, the second coxswain, was off duty, but not, at the moment, sleepy. He had taken his little set of pegged chessmen out of his locker before climbing into his bunk. Working out chess problems was a hobby, and a relaxation. But tonight there was an unusual noise which distracted him; each time *Thrasher* rolled there was a thump as if a heavy weight was moving from side to side.

It was the practice to relieve the look-outs at staggered intervals, so that two of the three men on the bridge were always fully accustomed to the darkness. Leading Seaman Adams, coming aft from his mess to the control room before going on the bridge to take over his watch, heard an unfamiliar clicking sound as he passed under the neighbourhood of the gun. Something was loose in the casing, the low superstructure outside the pressure hull overhead. Arrived on the bridge Adams reported what he had heard.

Mackenzie was on the bridge as well as the officer of the watch, Sub-Lieutenant Fitzgerald. Up there, with the bow-wave rustling by and the sea sluicing over the saddle tanks as the submarine rolled, nothing could be heard. Mackenzie sent Adams down on to the casing to investigate. The Leading Seaman dropped on to the cat-walk outside the conning tower and scrambled forward. On the side of the casing, just below the revolving gun

platform, was a large, jagged hole. Adams hurried back
to the bridge to report.

Mackenzie did some quick thinking. Clearly the hole
was the result of the aircraft attack twelve hours earlier.
Thrasher had sustained some damage, though it could
hardly be serious. But he wanted to know more. He sent
for his First Lieutenant, Lieutenant P. S. W. Roberts and
the Second Coxswain, Petty Officer Gould. Roberts was
his second in command and Gould was an experienced
man whose duties included the care of the casing. Very
shortly afterwards Roberts and Gould were down by the
gun. Here they made an alarming discovery. Lying on the
flat but narrow deck just in front of the shield of the four-
inch gun was quite a large bomb. It was three or four
feet long and six or seven inches in diameter. The tail
fins had been almost broken away, and as the submarine
rolled the bomb might at any moment slip off the casing
and fall on to the top of the saddle tank, with a jar which
would probably set it off. Gould did his best to steady
the bomb whilst Roberts hurried to report to Mackenzie.

As soon as he had heard the circumstances Mackenzie
turned *Thrasher* stern to the swell to stop her rolling.
The bomb must be got rid of as soon as possible. Sending
for one of the large sacks in which potatoes were supplied
Roberts returned to the casing.

By the look of it the bomb would weigh about 100
pounds, so two men could lift it without difficulty. But
the narrow casing, running down the centre-line of the
submarine, was bounded on either side by the top of
the pressure hull and the ballast tanks. The bomb could
not be dropped directly into the sea and was much too
heavy to be hurled clear. It would have to be carried into
the bow, a distance of about 100 feet.

Apart from its highly unpleasant contents the bomb
was an awkward object to handle, smooth and slippery
with sea water. Cautiously Roberts and Gould manoeuvred it into the sack. When this was done a heaving
line was passed around the bundle to give good hand-

holds. Lifting the bomb the two men began to make their way very carefully along the narrow casing towards the bow. The perforated steel deck was slippery. Half way to the bow it sloped upwards—a nasty little 'hill'. On this raised portion right forward the casing was cut away for the cables of the two anchors. There was not much foothold and the going, encumbered as they were with the bomb, was very difficult. Forward of this point the casing was very narrow indeed, but they were now beyond the end of the pressure hull with the sea at last directly below. The sack was lowered over the side, swinging just above the surface. When all was ready for the release Fitzgerald, standing half way along the casing as a link, informed the bridge. Mackenzie ordered *Thrasher's* motors 'half astern' and waited until the submarine had stern-way before giving the signal to let go. The bomb might be fitted with some hydrostatic device which the water pressure would operate, and he wished to get his ship as far away as possible in case it went off. The bomb splashed into the sea. Roberts and Gould scrambled aft away from the bow, very relieved that no explosion caught them a good deal too close to its source for their continued existence.

So far so good. But the bomb they had just got rid of had been lying on the casing *in front* of the gun and the jagged hole below the gun-platform was still unaccounted for. Roberts and Gould began to search the inside of the casing below the gun, shining a hooded torch through the flooding holes with which it was perforated. A second bomb was now discovered, lying on the pressure hull inside the circular trunk supporting the gun.

Mackenzie had a very nasty problem on his hands. This second bomb was extremely inaccessible. If he left it where it lay it might at any moment explode, and destroy the submarine. It must be disposed of, but how could this be done?

A few words of explanation about the construction of a submarine are necessary at this point. The submarine

proper is cigar-shaped, with a circular pressure hull, outside which, like the flaps of a saddle, are the ballast tanks.
To improve sea-keeping characteristics on the surface and
as an 'upper-deck', a narrow casing is built on top of
the hull extending from right forward, where it is bulbous
and comparatively high, to abaft the motor room. The
casing is of light plating about one eighth of an inch
thick, and only about two or three feet high for most of
its length. It is not water-tight and floods when the submarine dives. Various fittings which would destroy the
streamline shape of the submarine are located inside the
casing, the external torpedo tubes right forward and the
muffler tank or silencer for the diesel engines abaft the
conning tower. Elsewhere the space inside is encumbered
with pipes, valves, the framework of the casing itself and
other fittings. Equipment used in harbour and on the
surface such as ropes, fenders and the submarine's folding
boat are stowed inside the casing, access being provided by
a few hinged gratings.

The nearest of these was about twenty feet from the
place where the bomb had lodged, but the space between
was anything but clear. To get to the bomb a man could
not even crawl past the various obstructions on hands and
knees. He would have to lie flat, wriggling along as best
he could—a slow process at the best of times. It was 2.45
a.m. and a dark night. Men who had been on deck for
some time could pick out their surroundings, but inside
the casing the blackness was absolute. *Thrasher* was close
to a hostile coast and still not far from the place where
she had carried out a successful attack the day before. The
enemy would be looking for her, and at any moment she
might be forced to dive. No delay would be possible and
only those on the bridge would have time to get below. A
man left on deck might, if he was very lucky, survive
until he was picked up. In the casing he would have no
chance at all. The roar of the air gushing out of the ballast
tanks as the main vents were opened would be the signal
for a few agonising moments before he lost consciousness.

Roberts and Gould, knowing all this very well, calmly set about removing the second bomb. A second sack was sent for as the two men dropped down the grating and started to wriggle aft to the gun support twenty feet away.

Both these young men had a great deal to lose. Roberts, twenty-five, had joined the Navy as a cadet and had volunteered for submarines soon after war broke out. He was married. In the ordinary course of events he would be joining his wife and baby son in Portsmouth soon after the end of the patrol, for he was due for the 'periscope course' which officers undergo before being given their own command. His fair hair, blue eyes and good looks accounted for his nickname of 'Blondie', but he was a quiet, rather reserved young man.

The day before had been Gould's twenty-eighth birthday. He was a long-service Navy man who had been in submarines for nine years. Whilst *Thrasher* was 'working up' before sailing for the Mediterranean he had married a girl five years younger than himself. His wife was expecting a baby during the next few weeks. Gould was a cheerful chap, fond of boxing and swimming. His messmates called him 'Brighteyes'.

The two men, slowly making their way towards the bomb, were reasonably familiar with the inside of the casing. Both had stood by *Thrasher* when she was building. Gould's duties, as second coxswain, included the 'upper deck'. He was in charge of the men who worked the anchors and cables. Some of the gear used by his party was stowed in this part of the casing. He was responsible for painting it inside and had made the same journey in daylight, in harbour, on a number of occasions. Of course it was very different now, but the knowledge was a help.

They reached the bomb and examined it by the dim light of the screened torch. It seemed to be the same size as the one they had already disposed of. Although it had plunged through the side of the casing and made another jagged hole through the hollow gun support inside which

it now lay, it was in almost 'mint' condition. Its tail fins
were practically intact and the unpleasant looking
whiskers in its nose which operated the firing mechanism
unblemished. It was not jammed, but lying free. When
the submarine had been rolling it had been moving a
few inches from side to side, and it was this which had
made the sound first heard by Gould. Clearly the bomb
could not be passed out through the holes it had made.
It would have to be manoeuvred through the casing to
the grating.

The first stage of the journey was comparatively simple.
Immediately under the gun the casing was higher and
there was a large lightening hole in the gun support
through which the bomb could be passed. Gould slipped
into the support, lifted the bomb and handed it to
Roberts.

The bomb seemed to resent being disturbed. From its
interior came a twanging sound as though from a released
spring. Both men held their breath. Neither had the
knowledge to render their unpleasant companion 'safe'.
In such constricted surroundings it would be impossible
to avoid jolting it occasionally. True it had not exploded
when it hit the submarine, but bombs, as they knew,
were often fitted with a time-release which kept them safe
for a while. As gently as possible (which was not very
gently) Roberts laid it down on the deck.

Forward of this point the casing was very low. The
bomb could no longer be carried, or even lifted more than
a few inches above the pressure hull. Roberts and Gould
considered the matter and eventually hit on a plan.

Gould lay flat, feet pointing aft, with the bomb in his
arms. Roberts lay in front of him, head aft, pulling Gould
along by his shoulders and taking some of the weight of
the bomb. Between them they made a sort of human sled.
It was not a very rapid vehicle, but it worked. The way
was by no means clear, with many obstructions, and progress was painfully slow. The bomb was wet and slippery,
as was the top of the pressure hull on which they lay.

Water dripped from the casing above. The confined space smelt of salt and sea-slime, like the under-side of a seaside pier. Sometimes they had to use the torch, lighting momentarily the red-leaded interior of the casing, their own dirt-streaked faces and the inert, but somehow malevolent object within a few inches of their noses. Each time they jolted the bomb it gave the same disturbing 'twang' from its innards, and repetition made the sound no less alarming. Early in the journey the torch rolled out of reach. From that time they were in pitch blackness, feeling their way.

It took them about forty minutes to get the bomb those twenty feet and it seemed a very long time. Grunting and panting they struggled along. The sea splashed and gurgled as it washed over the saddle tanks. *Thrasher* pitched gently in the swell. On the bridge Mackenzie and the look-outs, powerless to help, swept the dark horizon with their glasses and hoped that no enemy would appear. The news of what was happening had quickly spread to all the men below. The thought of the explosion which might at any minute blow them to kingdom come was somehow less dreadful, because it was less easily imagined than another—the blare of the klaxon which would sound the last post for two messmates. Sydney Hart, serving in *Thrasher* at the time, wrote in his book* of the 'eerie silence' below, 'as if all hands were waiting for the usual depth-charge attack'.

At last the bomb was under the grating. Roberts and Gould looked up at the sky which they had been none too sure of ever seeing again. Fitzgerald was waiting for them with another sack. Now the bomb could at last be lifted and carried forward. After their struggles below the journey to the bow seemed simple, and before the bomb followed its fellow into the deeps Roberts insisted on delaying long enough to make a careful note of the various markings on the bomb casing (it was a 50 kg. bomb of German manufacture) which he felt might be useful to

* *Discharged Dead.* Sidney Hart. Odhams Press Ltd.

the Intelligence Services. When he had finished, *Thrasher* once more went astern and the bomb splashed into the sea. Roberts and Gould climbed on to the bridge. It was 3.40 a.m. and nearly two hours since the first bomb had been found.

At dawn *Thrasher* was in her new patrol area. A fortnight later she was back in harbour at Alexandria. The rest of the patrol was uneventful, but for once no one was sorry. Enough excitement had been crammed into twenty-four hours to last most men for a long time. In the sober words of the official report *Thrasher* had had a near-miraculous escape. Perhaps there was something in sailing on Friday the thirteenth after all.

In June 1942 Lieutenant P. S. W. Roberts and Petty Officer T. W. Gould were awarded the Victoria Cross.

CHAPTER NINE

MIERS AND *TORBAY*

A week after *Thrasher* had sailed for the patrol just described another 'T' class submarine of the First Flotilla left Alexandria. *Torbay*, Commander A. C. C. Miers, D.S.O. was bound for an area off the west coast of Greece between Levkas and Cephalonia, the focal point for shipping proceeding to and from the Gulf of Patras. On 24 February she was on her billet. The weather was vile, with a gale raising a very rough sea. Submarines, in spite of their low freeboard, are excellent sea-boats, but that night *Torbay,* on the surface charging her batteries, was badly 'pooped'. A great wave broke over the bridge from astern sending a cascade of water down the conning tower into the control room, some of which found its way into number three battery. Chlorine gas made men cough as they dealt with this emergency, but this was *Torbay's* tenth Mediterranean war patrol and her experienced crew soon had everything under control.

Torbay had arrived on the station in rather peculiar circumstances. She was at Portsmouth when every available submarine was suddenly ordered out for a special Biscay patrol. Half her crew was on long leave including the First Lieutenant, Engineer Officer and many key ratings. The vacancies were hurriedly filled by young and inexperienced men and *Torbay* sailed, afterwards proceeding direct to Gibraltar with the same very scratch crew. Miers himself had just returned to submarines after three and a half years in general service and the oldest of his executive officers was now only twenty-one. In spite of this *Torbay* sank two tankers and four small craft on her second patrol. On her third she accounted for the Italian submarine *Jantina*, a transport, a tanker and seven caiques. Miers and his *Torbay*, with anything but a flying start, soon established a reputation for aggressive efficiency. In November *Torbay* had landed a unit of No. 11 Commando on the North African coast, under very difficult conditions, for the gallant attack on Rommel's headquarters for which Lieut.-Colonel Keyes, son of Admiral of the Fleet Lord Keyes, was awarded a posthumous V.C.

Miers also came of fighting stock. His father, a Cameron Highlander, was killed in action in France in 1914. Tony Miers joined the Navy as a special entry cadet ten years later, volunteered for submarines in 1929 and was given his first command in 1936.

He followed firmly in the footsteps of the pioneers of the early days of submarines. No detail of his boat's construction or organisation escaped his prying eye. His standards were high, and he saw that they were meticulously observed. Outspoken and somewhat hot-tempered he might have been a very difficult man to serve, if his crew had not appreciated that strictures were applied even more fiercely to what he might consider were his own shortcomings. Though apparently impetuous his actions were closely reasoned. Over the years he had never lost sight of the fact that what he was preparing for was war. When the opportunity came, to quote the Captain commanding the flotilla, 'his sole ambition was to get at the enemy on every possible occasion.'

During her preceding patrol, in January, *Torbay* had spent several days off the coast of Crete, landing a small party of special troops. The weather was bad with a heavy surf on the beach originally selected. Miers patrolled the shore, looking for an alternative landing place; so close in that he could watch the local peasantry going to church (it was Sunday). The following night he surfaced and began the operation. One of the two folbots being used was damaged on the beach and the other holed as it bobbed up and down alongside the submarine. Miers decided to use a large rubber boat captured from a German

ship, but the 'Mauretania', as she had been christened by
his crew, developed a leak which took some hours to repair.
Next night he tried again; surfacing, loading the
'Mauretania' with her men and stores on the casing and
then partly-diving *Torbay* to float them off, a novel
manoeuvre which was accomplished 'without anyone going
overboard'. The 'Mauretania' was paddled ashore by some
of *Torbay's* crew, with orders to swim off to the submarine
if they could not manage the return journey against the
wind; this was happily unnecessary, but reflected the
determination of their commander. After some further
adventures with the 'friendly, but most frightened villagers'
all the troops were safely landed.

From Crete *Torbay* moved to the Gulf of Taranto
where she spent three fruitless days waiting for enemy
ships which never appeared. On the eleventh night of her
patrol she was recalled to Alexandria. The usual procedure
on passage was to dive from dawn to dusk. Miers calculated that, by remaining on the surface, he could save a
day and still arrive on time. Instead of starting for home
he closed to within fifteen miles of Taranto. The weather
was extremely clear and the approaches to the harbour
were all in view, but his luck was out and no targets
appeared. This was the immediate background to the
patrol just beginning.

On 26 February *Torbay* had surfaced after nightfall to
charge her batteries when she was told of a tanker
approaching her patrol area. The weather was still bad
with heavy showers of rain making life difficult for the
men keeping a look-out on the submarine's lurching,
wind-swept bridge. When the almost full-moon shone out
between the racing clouds, they could see quite well, but
during the squalls visibility was reduced to a few acres
of heaving, foam-capped sea. Miers, expecting to spend
most of the night on the bridge had, as was his custom,
ordered a pillow to be brought up so that he could snatch
a little rest propped up against the periscope standards
and remain instantly available; but at 2.0 a.m. he was on

his feet, peering into the darkness when the tanker appeared steering straight towards *Torbay* at slow speed. Five minutes later her escort could be distinguished, a single destroyer zig-zagging on the tanker's port bow.

Visibility at this moment was quite good and Miers decided that conditions were unsuitable for an attack from ahead. At 2.18 a.m. he dived, passed under the enemy and surfaced a quarter of an hour later astern of them. At full speed on both engines he followed up, trying to keep the tanker between *Torbay* and the destroyer. Driving rain and clouds blotting out the moon made it difficult to see the tanker and to judge distances. After being temporarily blinded by a squall Miers found himself so close to his target that he had to stop both engines to avert a collision. A torpedo at this range would not have time to pick up its depth, but when the tanker had drawn about 400 yards ahead he fired. *Torbay* was yawing badly in the rough sea. The torpedo missed, but its track was seen and the tanker began to flash a frantic message to the destroyer, which swivelled round to investigate. Unfortunately the moon, shining down behind *Torbay*, was unobscured. Miers put his helm hard over, trying to keep bows-on to the destroyer to present the smallest silhouette, but he was spotted. Still under full helm he dived.

The klaxon blared, the main vents opened and *Torbay* quickly began to slide under the surface. Miers, following the look-outs down the conning tower, tried to pull the upper hatch shut behind him, but it would not close. He just had time to let himself slip down the ladder and slam the lower hatch as water gushed into the conning tower. *Torbay* was already well under and the additional weight accelerated her progress. The First Lieutenant's (Lieutenant P. C. Chapman) efforts to correct the trim were not helped by the blare of the klaxons and the alarm, whose wiring in the flooded conning tower had been short-circuited. Both continued to fill the boat with a nerve-wracking din until their fuses were drawn. It was a test of the coolness and good training of the crew, but

Torbay levelled off successfully and was in trim again when the depth-charges began to explode. Eleven were recorded, but the rough sea must have handicapped the destroyer for only the first few were close enough to be really alarming. Three quarters of an hour later *Torbay* surfaced on an empty sea. Miers' anger at having missed the tanker was not soothed by the discovery that the upper conning tower hatch had been jammed by his own pillow, left on the bridge in the excitement of the attack. It was typical that this error was later duly recorded in his patrol report.

That afternoon he got the chance partly to make good when two small ships escorted by an armed trawler were sighted moving down the coast. None of them was worth a torpedo so *Torbay* surfaced and opened fire with her gun, quickly setting one of the supply ships ablaze. Her companion and the trawler turned shorewards, pursued by *Torbay* who continued the chase until put under by accurate fire from a coastal battery.

On the night of 1 March *Torbay* was patrolling on the surface. The sea had gone down, but rain-squalls made the visibility rather variable. As one of these squalls passed away it revealed a *Clio* class destroyer only about a mile away. *Torbay* tried to keep end-on to the destroyer, for even on the surface submarines can be very hard to see, but she was sighted before she had dived. She immediately went deep and the depth-charges were soon crashing off, the first seven being unpleasantly close. *Torbay*, with every unnecessary piece of machinery stopped, stole along as quietly as possible as she tried to anticipate the enemy's moves. Her own asdic set told her that the destroyer had been joined by another A.S. vessel and the two continued to hunt the submarine and to drop depth-charges for nearly an hour before they lost contact. After an interval *Torbay* came up to see two destroyers still searching, but some distance off.

The weather had now taken a very decided turn for the better and the next night was uneventful, with a calm sea and a bright moon. The sun came up; patrolling aircraft occasionally passed over the cloudless sky, but nothing appeared on the blue horizon until 5.30 p.m. when a single ship was reported. Steering straight for *Torbay* as she swam along at periscope depth was a *Curtatone* class destroyer. She was steaming slowly, at 12 knots, not zig-zagging, but sweeping—a routine sweep, for she certainly had not sighted *Torbay*. Miers decided it was too good an opportunity to miss, ordered the six torpedoes in the bow tubes to be set to run shallow, and started his attack, intending to fire from the destroyer's starboard side. Half an hour later he was still unobserved, 800 yards off the enemy's track and almost abeam. Putting the periscope up for a quick look as he swung *Torbay* to starboard to fire Miers saw that the destroyer had altered course and was coming straight towards him, forcing him to go deep, though still he did not think he had been sighted. Two minutes later the destroyer rumbled by overhead. As the sound of her passing faded there was a series of six 'simply deafening reports'. *Torbay* was lifted bodily for several feet and very badly shaken. The shock smashed a number of gauges and other small fittings. The hatch over the engineer's store rose into the air and fell back with a crash. Inside the store was chaos, but all the essential parts of the submarine continued to function. Miers, with considerable experience of such matters, reported later that he had never had depth-charges so close, but he and his crew remained perfectly steady and calm, going through the familiar motions of taking avoiding action in the short lull whilst their enemy swung round in a half circle for another attack. It came eight minutes later, but this time the effect of the charges, though noisy and unpleasant, was not quite so violent. Further charges fell fairly close, but the enemy had now lost contact. *Torbay* crept away. It was her third encounter with enemy destroyers in three days and Miers decided to move to the other end of his patrol area, near Paxoi Island. It was a striking tribute to the mutual confidence

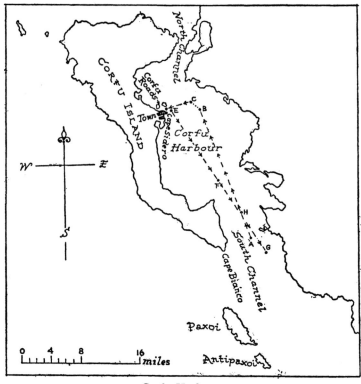

Corfu Harbour.

Explanation of Symbols

A: 1942/4: Surfaced and proceeded into Strait.

H: 2018/4: Forced to dive on sighting merchant ship coming up astern.

B: 2158/4: Reached position for charging batteries stern on to moon.

C: 0058/5: Estimated position at end of charge, due to westerly set.

D: 0235/5: Position in Corfu roads when no target other than destroyer visible; had to retire eastwards until dawn broke.

E: 0730/5: Firing position after which course was set at high speed to southeast.

F: 0930/5: Halfway to entrance came to periscope depth to check position.

G: 1120/5: Clear of Strait. Resumed patrol at periscope depth and continued on course for Alexandria.

which existed between Captain and crew that everyone was as cheerful and keen as ever, though fully aware that the enemy, forewarned of their presence, would now be very much on the alert, with every available A.S. vessel at sea.

Next day *Torbay* heard the 'pings' of probing destroyers, but none of them made contact. When night fell she surfaced as usual to charge her batteries. At 6.30 a.m., when the darkness was just beginning to give way, she sighted a small convoy; two single-funnelled ships escorted by aircraft and a destroyer. The weather was calm and clear and the convoy was some distance off. Miers closed them at full speed on the surface until the coming dawn forced him to dive. The convoy's course had been difficult to estimate in the half-darkness and *Torbay* was still a long distance off its track. Miers continued to chase at high speed submerged, but at 8.0 a.m. he realised that there was no chance of getting within range and abandoned the attack, after taking rather a lot out of his battery to no purpose.

The sun was now well up. It was a beautiful day. Even through the periscope you could see for miles. At 9.25 a.m. the masts and funnels of several ships steaming in company appeared over the horizon. It was a convoy of large ships, moving northward parallel to the coast.

Torbay's fruitless hunt after the earlier convoy had taken her south and west and she was now some distance out at sea, broad on the bow of the new convoy's mean line of advance. At full speed *Torbay* made to intercept, but she was still over five miles away fifty-five minutes later. It was too far off to fire, but the convoy was now clearly visible, four troopships escorted by three destroyers with two aircraft circling overhead. It was even possible to identify individual ships; the *Liguria*, 15,400 tons, the *Romolo*, 9,800 tons, the *Tevere*, 8,400 tons and the *Galileo*, 8,000 tons. It was a submariner's dream of a target, but unrealisable. *Torbay*, with her battery now very low, had no chance of closing the range. To sharpen the disappointment

the convoy had passed close to the place where *Torbay*
would have been patrolling if she had not gone off after
the other, and much less valuable ships, earlier. Miers,
furious with himself for having made what hindsight indicated had been an error of judgment, was frustrated, but
not defeated.

For most men the decision of what to do next would
have been an easy one. The battery was low; the convoy
disappearing over the horizon. When darkness fell *Torbay*
could surface, re-charge her battery, and hope for better
luck on the morrow. This was the safe, and indeed the
obvious course to follow. But Miers was thoroughly
aroused. Convoys like the one he had just seen were few
and far between. He refused to accept defeat.

'Knowing Commander Miers well, as I do,' wrote
Captain S. M. Raw of the First Submarine Flotilla later,
'it is clear that (he) was extremely angry with himself,
quite unjustifiably. Such a situation invariably arouses
Commander Miers' 'worst instincts' and determines him to
retrieve what he considers to be an error.' With the chart
in front of him Miers considered what he might do.

The Italians were always short of oil and the convoy
was steaming quite slowly, to economize fuel. The course
they were following, close inshore, would presently bring
them to the southern entrance of the harbour of Corfu,
stretching for thirty miles between the island of Corfu
and the mainland. The presence of a hostile submarine in
the neighbourhood would be known to them. In the
circumstances they would be safest in the open sea, with
plenty of room for manoeuvre. Why had they chosen to
abandon this advantage? The convoy would enter the
southern entrance before dark; what would it do next?
If it passed straight through he might be able to intercept
north of Corfu on the following day, by getting far enough
out to sea to surface and charge the battery during the
night and then moving east and north at full speed on
the diesel engines. But it was illogical of the convoy to
skirt the coast without good reason. It seemed to Miers

highly probable that it intended to anchor in the Corfu Roads. Intelligence had suggested that these Roads were being used as an assembly and fuelling point. The Italians must intend to remain for a while in the well-protected harbour, far from the open sea. Perhaps they would sail again at dawn, when the air escort was again available. Miers decided to follow them in and attack by moonlight. But first he must charge *Torbay's* almost exhausted battery.

Corfu Roads were about forty miles from *Torbay's* present position, half-way up the 30-mile long harbour so often used by the British Mediterranean Fleet before the war. Miers planned to approach the southern entrance during the day, and pass through the channel after dark but before moonrise. He had no exact information about the harbour defences, but controlled minefields and a deep, submerged obstruction in the channel were to be expected. The southern channel, five miles long, was four miles wide, but the Bianco Shoal, extending south and east of Corfu Island, reduced its effective width for a submarine to two and a half miles. Inside the harbour plenty of patrol vessels of all kinds must be available, and the local defence flotilla would now be reinforced by the three destroyers with the convoy. The enemy knew of a submarine in the vicinity and would be on the *qui vive*, but *Torbay* would have to spend at least three hours *on the surface* charging her batteries before attacking. The chart showed a number of secluded bays on the mainland side of the harbour proper which were unlikely to be heavily patrolled at night, but all of them were too far from Corfu town to allow *Torbay* to keep the Roads under observation. During those three hours the convoy might slip away through the north channel. Miers decided to make for a spot quite near the town, keeping, as he hoped, just far enough away to remain unobserved as he charged. Although the moon was almost full, a submarine with the dark mainland behind it would be hard to see. It was a simple, carefully conceived but very daring plan.

For the rest of the day *Torbay,* at slow speed, closed the southern channel, sighting only the usual air patrols, none of which spotted the dim shape of the slowly moving submarine. When darkness had fallen Miers surfaced near the Sicola light. It was so calm and still that *Torbay's* engines would be audible some way off, so he made the first part of the passage up the channel on his motors. He had not gone very far when a small vessel was sighted astern, also passing up the channel. Miers dived, let her overtake him, and followed her in. When she was well ahead he surfaced again, charging on one engine and propelling with the other. Just before 10.0 p.m. he was in the position he had selected, opposite the town of Corfu on Cape Sidero, but about five miles offshore. Both engines were now used to charge the battery. Miers was careful to keep *Torbay's* stern to the very bright moon hanging high in the sky over the dark outline of the Grecian shore. The ballast tanks were partly flooded and the low silhouette of the conning tower should be difficult to distinguish against the loom of the land.

For nearly three hours the diesels chugged away, pumping precious amps back into the battery, but just before 1.0 a.m. on 5 March a patrol vessel approached from the west. In the bright moonlight Miers feared he must have been seen as he hurriedly dived. For a quarter of an hour he watched the patrol which had stopped her engines and was lying not far off. The patrol began to move, but turned away. At 1.35 a.m. she had disappeared. The First Lieutenant now reported that the battery was fairly well up, so Miers decided to remain under and close the Roads.

The next hour as *Torbay* stole across the harbour, was a tense one. The lights of the northern entrance suddenly came on, to admit a merchant ship from the north. When she had entered the Roads they went out again. A little later a motor launch was sighted. Like the other patrol vessel she approached, stopped her engines and seemed to be listening. *Torbay,* going dead slow on one motor, crept by. Five minutes later the sound of two small explosions were clearly heard. Miers decided that this was a routine matter; charges dropped in the anchorage, now close at hand, against the possibility of attacking frogmen or human torpedoes. At 2.35 a.m. *Torbay* was half a mile from Cape Sidero and actually in the Roads, rather sooner than planned because of an unexpected westerly set of the tide. Although the moon was still up it was too dark to see properly through the periscope. The ships anchored in the Roads were invisible against the dark shadow of the blacked-out town, behind which loomed Mount St. Giorgio. After almost ramming a destroyer, seen at the very last moment when the rays of the setting moon lit up the camouflage on her side, Miers decided he must wait until the light improved, so he turned round and withdrew eastward. He would attack in the twilight before dawn. This would mean passing out of the south channel in daylight. The air patrols would be up, but he hoped they would not be too active at such an early hour.

For four hours *Torbay* waited, dodging the many patrols which loomed up suddenly as they went about their business. 'A fairly harassing experience', wrote Miers in his report, in a magnificent understatement. It was very dark when the moon had set. Sometimes the patrols could be dimly seen; sometimes the only indication of their presence was a report from Petty Officer Telegraphist E. K. Kember on the listening gear. More small charges were dropped in the Roads between 3.0 and 3.30 a.m. A quarter of an hour later the north channel lights went on again for a while to admit another ship. In constant vigilance the hours dragged by until shortly before 6.0 a.m., when Miers decided it was light enough to have another try. He was approaching the Roads on a firing course when a patrol vessel suddenly appeared at high speed and almost rammed *Torbay*. Miers went deep and turned in a circle to try once again.

The sum of these delays meant that the attack would now have to be carried out in broad daylight. Conditions were extremely difficult, with a glassy calm sea, patrol craft all around and possibly aircraft overhead. Miers, accepting all these risks, closed in for the third time and cautiously raised his periscope. There were two rowing boats moving slowly across very close at hand. Next time he looked the field of view was clear; the Roads, the town, Mount St. Giorgio, but the convoy had gone.

It was a bitter blow; but the Roads were not quite empty. Lying quietly at anchor, beam on, were two supply ships of about 8,000 and 2,000 tons. A single destroyer, at anchor or underway, was with them, but swung at a different angle. Miers fired six torpedoes, two at each ship. As *Torbay* went deep to make her get-away the crew heard the explosion of two hits. Both the merchantmen had been torpedoed, though the destroyer was missed.

The explosions were the signal for the outbreak furious activity in the harbour. Patrol craft rushed about, but none of them had seen *Torbay*, now moving at full speed towards the south channel. Fortunately at this early hour (7.30 a.m.) the surprised defence was unco-ordinated. *Torbay*, cautiously coming to periscope depth twenty-five minutes later, saw various craft searching in the position from which she had fired, but none in pursuit. The destroyer was underway, but some distance astern. An aircraft was circling, but over the anchorage. Depth-charges were being dropped in large numbers, but none fell close. All this was satisfactory, but *Torbay* still had the narrow exit channel to negotiate. It was lucky for her that the enemy made up his mind that the submarine was still in the harbour. Before *Torbay* gained the open sea, nearly four hours after firing the torpedoes, she passed two patrol vessels, both hurrying back to Corfu. There was a final scare when a schooner seemed to be trying to drag some sort of a net or obstruction across the channel ahead, but *Torbay* was in the clear south of Sicola Island by 11.20 a.m., seventeen hours after she had passed the same spot the evening before. Ten minutes later she sighted an A.S. trawler, but as *Torbay*'s battery was nearly flat Miers for once decided not to attack. The machine was practically run down and so was the crew, the most responsible members of which had now been on duty almost continuously for over twenty-four hours. But just over an hour later, when a supply schooner hove in sight, Miers had recovered his form. Ordering 'Gun Action Stations', he prepared to surface. The schooner's life was saved by an aircraft which now appeared overhead. When it had moved away the schooner was safely entering Gayo Harbour. *Torbay* continued on patrol, surfacing after dark to charge her 'almost exhausted battery'. Her log shows 14 hours 59 mins. submerged on 4 March followed by 18 hours 27 mins. on the 5th. The battery had certainly served them well!

This should have been the last day of *Torbay*'s patrol, but during the night orders were received telling her to proceed at once to the Gulf of Taranto instead of returning to Alexandria. The news, as Miers remarked, 'was not received with quite the customary enthusiasm.' It was not until 18 March, after spending twenty-six unusually active days at sea, that she finally secured alongside the depot ship *Medway*. The ships of the Italian Fleet which she had been sent to intercept were never sighted, but the five days' extension to the patrol were not without its excitements. On 13 March it was seen that a torpedo in one of the upper deck tubes had sheered its securing stops and was lolling, half in and half out of the tube. The fan on the pistol of the warhead had revolved so the torpedo was fully armed, and would certainly resent rough treatment. The Engineer Officer, Lieutenant (E) H. A. Kidd, standing on the slippery saddle-tank up to his waist in water, tried to lever it gently out with a crow-bar, but the torpedo would not budge. Eventually Miers got rid of it by trimming down, going astern and firing the tube, an unavoidable waste of a torpedo which he much resented.

On the way back to Alexandria from south of Calabria *Torbay*'s crew, somewhat debilitated by the experiences of the last few weeks, was smitten with an epidemic of colds and influenza. The coxswain, Acting Chief Petty Officer H. C. F. Baker, did his best for them, but a number of the men were really ill. In spite of this, Miers made a small detour to the waters off Benghazi looking for targets. He was never satisfied so long as he had a torpedo left or a few rounds of gun ammunition remaining.

This was *Torbay*'s penultimate patrol before returning to the U.K. to refit. She sailed again early in April, sank a minesweeper by gunfire on the 9th and a laden schooner two days later. On 18 April she attacked a 5000-ton merchant ship and sank her with two torpedoes, evading the counter-attack of her escorting destroyer. The patrol was now nearing its end, but on 21 April *Torbay* was diving off Crete when she sighted a petrol carrier steaming along the coast. It was a ship of about 1400 tons, flying the German naval ensign; probably of rather too shallow draft for a torpedo, but armed with an A.A. gun in the bow, a 4-inch or 4.7-inch gun amidships, a small gun aft and machine guns on the bridge. Miers thought he might miss her with a torpedo and decided on gun action in spite of this quite formidable battery.

He surfaced on her quarter about a mile away and closed at full speed on his main motors. *Torbay*'s gun misfired, as the enemy turned flashing a challenge. Miers told Corporal J. Booth of the Seaforth Highlanders, his folbot-man, who was standing on the bridge with a Bren gun at the ready, to hold his fire, and got off the first round whilst the enemy was still debating whether the submarine was friend or foe. This first shot by Able Seaman L. A. Phillips, who had already sunk twenty ships with *Torbay*'s four inch gun, blew the enemy's midship gun over the side. Booth now made good shooting with the Bren, flattening the crew of the forward gun. As *Torbay* scored further direct hits the men round the enemy's after gun began to jump over the side as the petrol carrier caught fire, sending up a great cloud of black smoke which was seen from the shore. Large shells zoomed overhead and cracked into the sea near *Torbay* as heavy batteries opened up. As the submarine hurriedly dived, two German M.A.S. craft appeared and started a hunt, but Miers shook them off. This was *Torbay*'s last action in the Mediterranean with Miers in command, a spirited finale to a spectacular year.

There is an interesting and typical tailpiece. In July 1942, Miers was summoned to the Palace to be invested with his Victoria Cross. Three of his officers were to receive D.S.O.'s and D.S.C.'s, but the decoration of twenty-four ratings with the C.G.M. was indefinitely postponed. Miers immediately joined battle with the Lord Chamberlain's Office. Politely, but extremely firmly he informed them that his medical advisors would insist that his health would not allow him to wait upon His Majesty—unless he could be decorated with the rest of his crew. Surprise is one of warfare's most valuable weapons and the flabbergasted Lord Chamberlain eventually gave way. He was to suffer a further reverse. Awards are presented in a strict order of precedence. The Victoria Cross comes first, followed by such distinctions as the O.M. and K.C.B., with the D.S.O. and D.S.C. some way down the list and the C.G.M. further still. On the day of the Investiture, protocol was heavily and permanently dented, this time, no doubt, with King George VI's approval. Except for other recipients of the Victoria Cross, the procession into the Throne Room was headed by Miers and his men.

CHAPTER TEN

LINTON:
PANDORA AND *TURBULENT*

IN September 1939 there was a large British submarine flotilla on the China Station. The 'O', 'P' and 'R' classes of which it was composed were very much alike—ocean-going submarines of over 2000 tons unsuitable for the shallow waters of the North Sea. At first they were not recalled, but when Italy entered the war and France fell there was an urgent requirement for submarines in the Mediterranean. The First Submarine Flotilla was formed at Alexandria from the China submarines and a few large minelayers sent out from England. None of these big boats was really suitable for the very difficult conditions—clear, confined waters ringed by a hostile coastline and heavily patrolled; but it was Hobson's choice.

In May 1940 *Pandora*, Lieutenant Commander J. W. Linton, reached Suez from the Far East. Early in June she sailed for the Aegean on her first war patrol. Although glad to be in action at last Linton, like his brother commanding officers, realised that *Pandora* was by no means ideal for the duties she must now perform. The 'O', 'P' and 'R's were more than twice the size of the 'U' class and a good deal bigger and more clumsy than a 'T' boat, slower to dive and less handy under water. To give them very high surface endurance for ocean warfare they carried a great deal of oil. The fuel tanks were *outside* the pressure hull, and it had been found impossible to keep them absolutely oil-tight. Bulk and a lack of manoeuvrability made such big submarines a comparatively easy target; to make matters worse they sometimes left a tell-tale 'slick' of oil on the surface. The hull,

designed for a diving depth of 200 feet as against the 300
feet of later classes, was more vulnerable to heavy attacks,
and the captain had less choice of depth when dodging
depth-charges. On the credit side they were well armed,
with six bow and two stern tubes and a 4-inch gun. The
really useful speed of 18 knots on the surface would be a
great help for overtaking convoys at night or for proceeding quickly to a new patrol position. By submarine
standards they were roomy and comfortable, valuable
assets on a long patrol. But they were getting old. Built
in the 1930's they suffered from a tendency, current at
that time, of being unduly complicated. Maintenance was
always a heavy item and reliability not as great as it should
have been. It was fortunate that their crews were very
experienced and that their commanding officers had many
years of submarining behind them, men like 'Tubby'
Linton who knew all the tricks of 'the trade'.

John Wallace Linton was thirty-five years old, a
regular naval officer and an exceptionally good example
of an easily recognisable type. He had joined the Navy as
a cadet, passing through Osborne and Dartmouth without
much academic distinction, though the boy who used to ask
his mother to set him sums to pass the time when laid up
by some childish illness, showed a considerable flair for
mathematics. Physically very robust, with a good eye and
plenty of guts he was soon playing rugger for the First XV.
Later when he was again ashore doing the courses for
Lieutenant he was selected to play for the Navy. Young
ladies visiting Twickenham with their boy-friends might
have been more taken by the spectacular efforts of the three-
quarters and halves, but those who really knew the game
recognized in Linton a forward of distinction, a very
useful member of the pack, quick to seize an opportunity
and with a knack of being in the place where he was most
needed. When in 1937 he gave up first class rugger he
played a good deal of golf. He had a terrific drive, but it
was his short game—unflustered, carefully planned—

which often brought him victory. Linton at play had given a preview of how he would fight a war.

He joined submarines in 1927 and worked his way steadily through the less responsible posts of 'third hand' and first lieutenant, where his superiors found him most reliable. The ratings quickly recognized an officer with whom no liberties could be taken. He was liked and respected by juniors and seniors; in fact an excellent officer. Those who knew him best recognized something which set him a little above his fellows; unusual determination; common-sense with a touch of genuine inspiration; quiet courage in an emergency which automatically made him the leader. He was a steadfast man, never leaving a job half done however boring or trivial it might be. His powers of concentration were exceptional and he could add up a column of figures almost at a glance. He played a good hand at bridge and was a voracious if rather indiscriminating reader; but his great hobby was mathematics.

In due course he passed the 'perisher' or periscope course and was given his first command. He was happily married, with two small sons, and at home very much of a family man. There was nothing small about Linton himself. Like other ageing athletes he had put on weight and now tipped the scales at seventeen stone. The big, black beard which he had also grown (it sprouted luxuriantly without the least difficulty as soon as he stopped shaving) added to his imposing appearance. As he was not very tall his nickname of 'Tubby' was highly appropriate. The beard put the seal on what had long been apparent; Tubby Linton was a character, the sort of man whom people like to claim as a friend and to tell little stories about. *Pandora,* which he commanded, was an efficient and satisfied ship, because his crew had complete confidence in him. The flotilla as a whole regarded him as one of its very best commanding officers.

At the end of June, Britain with her back to the wall, was faced with the highly disagreeable task of ensuring that the French Fleet did not fall into German hands. *Pandora* was ordered to patrol off Algiers and on 3 July Linton was instructed to attack any French warships he encountered. Next day he sighted the minelaying sloop *Rigault de Genoully*. The conditions were unfavourable for a successful attack with *Pandora* broad on the minelayer's bow, a long way off her track and steering an opposite course. Linton immediately increased to full speed, turned to close and fired four torpedoes nine minutes later, hitting with three of them at a range of 3800 yards. Technically it was a masterly performance though, in the sad circumstances of the time, without savour.

Returning to Gibraltar *Pandora* embarked some R.A.F. key personnel and badly needed spares for fighter aircraft. With every available space filled (the cargo included 102 bags of mail), *Pandora* and another submarine successfully inaugurated what came to be known as the 'magic carpet service' to Malta, which was to do such valuable work during the long siege. *Pandora* went on to Alexandria, patrolling on the way off Benghazi, where she attacked a supply ship. Her engines were giving trouble and a piston had to be changed, work which was done whilst she was diving.

The First Flotilla scored a number of successes, but the unsuitability of big ocean-going submarines for work in the Mediterranean was being tragically proved. Before the end of the year seven out of seventeen boats had been sunk by the enemy, but they had filled the gap until they could be replaced with 'T' boats, now coming into service in large numbers, and by the little 'U's based on Malta.

After carrying out five not very productive patrols in the Mediterranean *Pandora* was transferred to the newly formed 8th Submarine Flotilla based on Gibraltar on 31 December. For a very keen and capable submarine officer it was a dull assignment. During the next five months Linton carried out a successful patrol off Sardinia, sinking two ships, but spent most of his time in the Atlantic and

Bay of Biscay, sighting little of interest except a couple of distant U-boats. Submarines were attached to Atlantic convoys at this period of the war as some sort of a protection against enemy raiders, a dreary and unprofitable duty. By the end of May, *Pandora* had done 251 days at sea in just over a year, including 196 days on patrol. It was a very long time since she had had a refit. The battery needed renewal and other defects were accumulating. In June she was sent to the U.S.A. for a thorough overhaul at Portsmouth, New Hampshire. She eventually returned to the Mediterranean and did useful work running the 'magic carpet' service until she was sunk in an air raid on Malta on 1 April 1942. But Linton was no longer in command. On 18 November 1941 he commissioned one of the 'T' class submarines, whose name he was to make famous—*Turbulent*.

Turbulent left England on 3 January 1942, carried out a short 'working-up' patrol from Gibraltar and arrived at Malta on 2 February. Her first war patrol, in the Aegean, was uneventful. She arrived at Alexandria, where the First Submarine Flotilla was still based, on Friday 13 February; 'a date', as Captain S. M. Raw remarked, 'which I confidently predict will prove an unlucky one for the axis powers'.

Pandora had never been entirely suitable for the arduous work in the Mediterranean. With *Turbulent* in Linton's capable hands man and weapon were united. During his second war patrol of this series (Linton's 13th) he sank six small vessels by gunfire and escaped some heavy depth-charging, after an attack on a convoy, with only minor damage. With the convoy Linton was robbed of success with his torpedoes because he got in too close. The convoy was heavily escorted—four trawlers, three aircraft patrolling overhead and no less than four destroyers. After passing under one of the wing destroyers *Turbulent* came to periscope depth for a 'look', to find one of the trawlers only 100 yards ahead, in Linton's selected firing position. Linton tried again, but was once more baulked by a trawler this time only 50 feet away. He fired his stern tubes as he tried to open the range before the convoy passed out of reach, but the torpedoes missed. Some of the subsequent depth-charges fell 'pretty close', breaking a number of lights. 'This gratuitous and quite unprovoked (sic) insult', wrote Linton in his report 'will, I hope, shortly be avenged'.

Avenged it was in a long series of successful patrols in which *Turbulent* steadily added to her bag. About three weeks at sea would be followed by a fortnight in harbour for maintenance of machinery and to rest the crew. It was an arduous life for a man nearing forty—indeed, arduous enough for the much younger men forming *Turbulent's* crew; but all were upheld by two very important things—the feeling of success and their confidence in Tubby Linton, stout, caustic, imperturbable, rubbing his black beard as he waited for the periscope to hiss up for a quick look during an attack or as he gave his orders while *Turbulent* altered course and depth when the charges were crashing off.

Linton had a special position in the flotilla, and not only as the oldest and most experienced of the submarine C.O.'s. For fifteen years submarines had been his life. It was a life for which he was entirely suited and he had devoted his considerable gifts to studying its problems from every possible angle. He had evolved what might be described as his own philosophy, but he did not keep the fruit of his labours to himself. Without ever thrusting his views down anyone else's throat he was always willing patiently to help the less experienced, and he had a knack of doing this without pomposity or making others feel small. A father-figure, but a very successful parent.

But he was not an 'easy' man. Submarining was his life and he was somewhat intolerant of those engaged in other pursuits. He was outspoken and his reports were sometimes highly critical of what he considered stupidity or failure of 'lesser men without the law' who were not in the crew of an operational submarine. The criticisms were harsh, but usually well-founded. Long signals in code which had to be laboriously decyphered and whose sense could easily have been conveyed in a short message were a particular bugbear. 'A perfect example of cypher diarrhoea' is a typical comment.

His fourth patrol, in May and early June, was described by his superiors as 'outstandingly successful'. Captain P. Ruck Keen, who had now relieved Raw as Captain 'S', called it 'the work of an astute and skilled artist'.

Three days after leaving Alexandria he polished off a schooner laden with ammunition which exploded with a tremendous bang as *Turbulent* was put under by an aircraft. On 17 May Linton was on the surface at night when he sighted a convoy of two ships, escorted by a destroyer. He slipped in behind them and followed the dim shapes in the darkness, noting their alterations of course as they zig-zagged, and checking their speed. After about an hour he worked his way up on to their beam, still unobserved, and turned in to attack. Ranges are very difficult to estimate at night and he was still too far off as they drew ahead, so he patiently repeated the manoeuvre after once more overtaking them. This time he got within firing range, sent off three torpedoes and scored two hits. The destroyer immediately attacked and the upper conning tower hatch refused to close properly as *Turbulent* dived, but she dodged the depth charges without too much difficulty. On surfacing an hour later Linton had to use the gun tower hatch whilst the partly-flooded conning tower was being drained. 'The designers of this hatch cannot have visualised its rapid use by a C.O. of fairly advanced years who has not retained the slim figure of his early youth', remarks Linton drily.

On 24 May *Turbulent* was very nearly sunk by an aircraft which plastered her with bombs when she was still close below the surface. Two days later Linton was attacking an escorted convoy at night when he was spotted by a destroyer, although end-on. The destroyer was only just over a mile away when *Turbulent* dived and her first pattern of depth-charges went off 'uncomfortably close'. The destroyer swung round to drop another pattern, rumbling directly overhead as they went off: 'so it must have been fairly near'. Twenty-five charges were counted altogether.

But all this merely served to put Tubby Linton on his metal, and there was more than a week of the patrol to run. On the night of 28 May he surfaced, to charge the battery and look around for targets. It had been a hot, still day. The sea was flat-calm and mist had formed with the darkness, making visibility very variable. But for this it would have been possible to see a long way, for the moon was almost full.

At 10.0 p.m. some flares blazed up not far off, origin unknown. Linton had been running on his diesel engines, but he now stopped them. On the bridge men searched the misty horizon with their glasses. Down below other men were using their instruments to try to pick up propellor beats.

Shortly after 11.0 p.m. the look-outs sighted a small convoy; two ships escorted by two destroyers. The mist made it very difficult to see how far off they were and what course they were steering. Linton decided to shadow and attack at first light, or earlier by moonlight if the mist cleared. But first he must get into position ahead of the enemy, and do so without being seen. Half an hour later, when he had worked his way up on to their beam, the mist closed down, hiding them completely. He altered course in what he judged was the right direction (the convoy would surely be zig-zagging) and after twenty anxious minutes picked them up again.

Linton was now on the bow of the convoy's mean line of advance, and fairly close in. The convoy was zig-zagging about 20 degrees on either side of its true course. The times for altering course were irregular and the destroyers would "suddenly appear out of the mist and seem twice their size'.

For two hours he continued to shadow, waiting his

opportunity. At last, at 2.30 a.m., the mist seemed to have thinned. He decided to attack by moonlight. With a nearly full moon still overhead he would have to dive to get close enough to fire, but aircraft would almost certainly put in an appearance at dawn and might spoil the whole show. During the next hour or so he worked himself into a favourable position and dived, five miles ahead of the convoy and 3000 yards off what he reckoned was its mean line of advance. Seven minutes later he turned in on to what he hoped would be the firing course.

Visibility was very much worse than he had expected and the periscope kept clouding over. He had hoped his asdic operator would be able to hear the nearest destroyer manoeuvring on the convoy's bow, but for over a quarter of an hour—a very long time under such circumstances— he could neither see nor hear the enemy. Trusting in having made an accurate appreciation of their movements Linton held on, and was finally able to distinguish two dim shapes which he decided were the merchant ships. They had zigged towards and were closer than antici- pated. There was neither sight nor sound of the nearest destroyer, but it must be closer still.

Four long minutes had passed when the destroyer materialised out of the mist with startling suddenness. *Turbulent* was right in its track. Linton took a quick bearing of the rapidly approaching shape. Two minutes later he checked the bearing; it had not changed. This meant that the destroyer was on a collision course, and it was now very close. He had two more minutes to run before he could fire. If he held on he might be rammed, but if he went deep he would certainly miss what might be his only chance. Linton held on, watching the mer- chant ships sliding into range and the growing bulk of the approaching destroyer. As he gave the order to fire 'the destroyer looked revolting and occupied the entire peri- scope'. As soon as the four torpedoes had sped on their way *Turbulent* hurriedly went deep. 'I was extremely relieved to see 40 feet on the gauge and know we were safe from being rammed.'

The salvo had been 'spread' to try and cover both ships. The nearest was only 1200 yards away, and the first bang of a hit came in just over a minute. But a few seconds later there was another noise, evidently made by one of *Turbulent*'s own torpedoes running wild with gyro failure and passing directly overhead. Another bang indicated that the second and more distant merchant ship had been hit. Forty-two seconds later there was a third bang. The errant torpedo 'repenting of the fright it had caused' had hit the nearest destroyer as it circled round.

Depth-charges had been falling, but the counter-attack now petered out. One of the destroyers was busy picking up survivors from the merchant ships and the other, in a sinking condition, was otherwise engaged. When *Turbulent* surfaced soon after dawn the only ship in sight was a single destroyer, moving slowly amongst the wreckage three miles off.

The sinking of the fleet destroyer *Emmanivele Pessagno* had been a piece of luck and Linton was not on the whole a very 'lucky' man. He was a master of his craft and his many successes were due to skill; attacks pressed home in the face of great difficulties in which every move, like that of a great chess player, was correct. Technically he was probably the best of all the British submarine commanders of World War II. He had studied his profession so thoroughly and had such a quick, clear, mathematical brain, that he often was able to give the correct D.A.* for firing before the various instruments into which data had been fed produced the same result. What he lacked was that inspired sixth sense by which some military commanders are able to guess the unforeseen.

Linton though technically almost perfect, extremely courageous and entirely competent was without this attribute of genius. Had he possessed it he would not sometimes have been robbed of success by something which

* Director angle. How much ahead to aim to hit.

no one could have foreseen. 'Unlucky' is the more general term.

On his next patrol he had worked himself into a perfect position to attack an important convoy escorted by half a dozen destroyers and three aircraft. None of the aircraft was very close when he approached his firing position 1200-1500 yards off the convoy's track—an ideal position for a very courageous man. He was about to pass 'just ahead or under' a destroyer when a combination of the light and the clearness of the water revealed him, below periscope depth, to one of the aircraft—a most unusual occurrence. The aircraft dropped a marker and swooped to attack, and two destroyers closed in, raining down depth charges, which did a lot of minor damage. *Turbulent's* beautifully executed attack was ruined, though Linton took the disappointment philosophically. 'The noise appeared to excite the amorous instincts of the rats' he wrote in his report. 'Throughout the afternoon there were shrill screams of satisfaction behind the three-ply above my bunk.'

On his seventh patrol he sank a number of ships, but two others escaped him when a heavy rainstorm, moving over the sea like a gigantic water-spout, blotted out the target at the critical moment. When it cleared the ships were too far off. The tale of successes is important, but so are incidents like these.

But *Turbulent* was already a famous submarine. Officers and men drafted to her were proud of the appointment, though entering on their new duties with some trepidation—for Tubby Linton was not an easy man to serve. He was a strict disciplinarian whom nature had endowed with a formidable presence.

Once after a night attack on the surface his telegraphist had difficulty in passing the required enemy report. Linton ordered the Chief Petty Officer in charge to be brought to the control room, which was darkened except for a few dim, red lights. *Turbulent* was rolling and pitching in a very rough sea, and in this nautical purgatory the man waited, holding on to keep his feet. The descent of Tubby Linton's large, oilskin-clad frame from the bridge was a truly awe-inspiring sight. When he was angry the voice which issued from the great, black beard was not his least alarming attribute. Five minutes later the report had gone through. He was feared, but greatly respected and the confidence of his crew in his ability was absolute.

On her eighth patrol *Turbulent* had some particularly nasty moments when a very heavy depth-charge attack damaged the lines connecting the control room with the hydroplanes. The First Lieutenant, Lieutenant J. A. R. Troup, quickly had the 'planes operating again in local control, and the well-trained crew successfully dealt with other damage, but it was a close-run thing. Once or twice it had been observed that Linton was twining a short length of his beard between thumb and forefinger, a sign (the only one) that he was anxious. Doubtless he felt fear like the rest of them, but it was fear under such strict control that he continued to look perfectly impassive. Once, in a rare burst of confidence, he asked his First Lieutenant if he got crinkles in his finger nails after depth-charging. 'I get them. It's because you're scared stiff.'

On this eighth patrol, a change being notably almost as good as a rest, Linton gave his crew something new to think about by starting what was to become a regular feature—bombarding targets from close inshore. Whilst he was doing so he ran into some submerged wreckage, but extricated *Turbulent* by diving out astern. Later he drove a ship ashore by gunfire and broke her back with a torpedo.

This patrol, from 28 October to 2 December 1942, was *Turbulent*'s longest, nearly 35 days in always dangerous waters. It was Linton's 19th war patrol and though his strong physique seemed unaffected he was a grimmer man than he had been when he had begun to play this most dangerous of all games eighteen months before. As Captain S. W. Roskill says in his official history, 'The War at

Sea', 'only a man of exceptional strength of character could have stood the strain of patrol after patrol.' Lesser folk subjected to such stresses have to force themselves to retain the necessary aggressive outlook. With Linton it had gone the other way; getting at the enemy had become almost an obsession. As in his old days on the rugger field his one idea was to seek out and tackle the foe.

Calling in at Malta on 4 November to pick up his orders for the Allied landings in North Africa he was asked by Captain G. W. G. Simpson if he would like to remain for a day or so in harbour, which the programme would allow. Linton shook his head. 'No thanks. I find it useless to be anywhere but at sea whilst the war is on. There are no targets here.' *Turbulent* sailed within four hours of entering harbour.

Turbulent had done 199 strenuous days on war patrol when she completed her first year in the Mediterranean. After two more patrols she was due to return to England for a refit.

Shortly after sailing on his penultimate patrol Linton sighted an important convoy escorted by two M.L.'s, three destroyers and no less than twelve aircraft. He pressed home his attack and torpedoed a ship of about 10,000 tons, escaping the inevitable depth-charges with his usual skill. Two days later he hit a 5000-ton ship with both torpedoes fired at her, and saw her sink. On 5 February at 4.45 a.m. he spotted a tanker escorted by three destroyers in the darkness, shadowed from ahead until just before dawn, dived and sank her at first light, hearing the ship break up as he was dodging the counter-attack half an hour later. Targets continued to be plentiful, but during the next few days *Turbulent* was baulked of her prey so Linton closed the land and bombarded a train standing in St. Ambroglio Station from 2100 yards, scoring several hits including one on the engine. 'E' boats rushed to the spot and *Turbulent* 'had a good deal of broken glass.'

Admiral Sir Andrew B. Cunningham, C.-in-C., Mediterranean, described it as 'a valuable and productive patrol', but Linton himself was dissatisfied. Several targets had escaped him for one reason or another and he had missed a 'sitting' shot at an armed water-carrier in what he described in his report as 'a very bad attack'. 'Commander Linton criticizes himself', said another senior officer, 'but in an area which appears to have been 'alive' with E-boats and aircraft, his successes speak volumes for his skill and experience.'

If Linton had seen their expressions of praise it is doubtful if he would have been impressed. He was now most anxious to bring his score of ships sunk to 100,000 tons, and time was running short. However, he enjoyed himself in Algiers where the flotilla was now based and where the arrival of his well-known bearded figure in a night-club was greeted by the management with deference not unmixed with apprehension.

'*Turbulent* is now carrying out her last patrol before sailing to the U.K. to refit', wrote Captain G. B. H. Fawkes late in February 1943.

Linton had been allotted an area he knew, and liked, in the Tyrrhenian Sea. He sank a ship off Bonifacio on 1 March and fired at another off Bastia ten days later. He was to spend a fortnight south-west of Naples and had asked if he could afterwards proceed to Giglio Island, and then north-east. A heavy counter-attack had followed the incident on 11 March, but *Turbulent* was duly sighted off the east coast of Corsica on the 14th. She was expected to report on 18 March when off Sardinia, but Fawkes was not particularly disturbed when no message came through. He had reason to believe that the first part of *Turbulent*'s patrol had not been very fruitful and if Linton had been unable to fire all his torpedoes he would hang on, in an area where he must keep wireless silence, until the last possible moment. His orders gave him some latitude in this respect. He had been told to withdraw on 18 March and two days later Fawkes signalled the route *Turbulent* should follow from Sardinia to Algiers. These instructions called for an acknowledgement, but there was again no reply. On 24 March when the silence had continued for six days, it was clear that Tubby Linton and his gallant crew had gone.

What had happened can only be surmised. On 17 March an Italian communiqué had claimed that an 'enemy submarine had exploded after striking one of our mines.' There was a controlled minefield around Maddalena, on the northern tip of Sardinia. Linton had reconnoitred the entrance to Maddalena on his previous patrol and plotted the movements of the Italian minesweepers in the channel. He knew that two heavy cruisers were lying in the harbour. He was, in Fawkes' words, 'far too experienced to be rash' and had a very healthy respect for mines, but he was never the one to neglect an opportunity. None of the A.S. vessels or aircraft against whom he had so often matched his skill claimed him, but minefields can sometimes be out of position. Chance and not the enemy had perhaps defeated him in the end.

Admiral Sir Andrew Cunningham forwarded the last report on the famous *Turbulent* 'with very deep regret', speaking of 'the very great blow which will be long felt by us all.' This was no form of words. Like the loss of David Wanklyn eleven months before, also on his last patrol, it was a tragedy. Tubby Linton had been, as Commander A. C. Miers V.C., D.S.O. wrote to Mrs Linton, 'the mainspring and inspiration of the whole flotilla'. It is again no form of words to say that his death was a shock to the whole Submarine Service. 'I remember being absolutely shattered', wrote one of his old officers who had left *Turbulent* to take up another appointment' '—so great was my confidence in his ability and infallibility'.

In *Pandora* and *Turbulent* Linton had completed twenty-one long war patrols, by far the majority of them in the narrow seas which claimed 46 of the 74 British submarines sunk during the war. Between June 1941 and March 1943 he had been at sea on patrol for over 460 days, or nearly one day in two. He had sunk two warships

and 27 supply ships and damaged many others. The
Axis tonnage which Linton destroyed was only exceeded
by one other submarine C.O., Wanklyn.

In awarding the Victoria Cross, in May 1943, to this
very brave and extremely skilful man the citation includes
these words.

'From the outbreak of war until H.M.S. *Turbulent's*
last patrol Commander Linton was constantly in command of submarines and during that time inflicted
great damage on the enemy. . . . In his last year he spent
two hundred and fifty four days at sea, submerged for
nearly half the time, and his ship was hunted thirteen
times and had two hundred and fifty depth charges
aimed at her.

'His many and brilliant successes were due to his
constant activity and skill, and the daring which never
failed him when there was an enemy to be attacked.'

CHAPTER ELEVEN

CAMERON AND PLACE

THE conquest of Norway in 1940 gave the Germans
bases from which their heavy ships could menace the
trade routes of the North Atlantic. When convoys to
North Russia began to run in 1941 the threat was
accentuated. Admiral Sir Max Horton, the Flag Officer,
Submarines, had long been considering how these enemy
battleships and battle cruisers could be attacked. Their
anchorages, at the heads of the many fiords in the lace-like
Norwegian coastline, were far from the open sea, out of
reach of surface ships or conventional submarines and
beyond the range of the R.A.F.'s heavy bombers. It was
impossible for our own battlefleet to remain constantly
on patrol to catch them on their rare sorties. They must
be got at where they spent most of their time, in harbour,
but how could this be done? Horton approved the design
for a midget submarine which could penetrate the nets
and other defences, and his successor, Admiral Sir Claud
Barry, enthusiastically followed up the plan.

The novel principle on which these little craft were
armed was conceived by a retired officer, Commander C
Varley D.S.O., R.N., and the first midget was built on
the Hamble River by his small firm, Varley Marine. X 3,
as she was called was launched in March 1942. Her trials
were promising and in May an order was placed with
Vickers-Armstrongs Ltd., the most experienced submarine-
builders in the country, for six operational X-craft.

They were to be 50 feet long with a pressure hull only
five feet six inches in diameter. A single small diesel
engine gave a surface speed of 6½ knots, and an electric
motor 4½ knots maximum when submerged. The battery
was comparatively big—sufficient for over 100 miles at
slow speed. Ordinary submarines in miniature, but with

168

one very unusual feature. Each little X-craft would carry as much high explosive as a full salvo from the ten tubes of a 'T' class submarine thirty times as large. But an X-craft carried no torpedoes. They would creep under their target as it lay at anchor in shallow water and deposit very large explosive charges on the sea-bed, fired by time-clocks. The comparatively soft 'under-belly' of a ship is always one of its weakest points and these charges, or side-cargoes as they were called, each contained two tons of amatol. Two were carried, slung on either side of the hull like the flaps of a saddle—enormous things looking almost as big as the midget itself.

The interior of the 'X' craft was nearly filled by its machinery, and very cramped. It was divided into four compartments, the fore-end, in which the battery was stowed, the so-called wet and dry or W & D compartment, of which more later, the control room and the engine and motor room. The crew was originally two officers and one rating. The control room was the only place where a small man could stand upright, under a low dome on the hull five feet six inches from the deck. A single small periscope, which could be raised and lowered in the ordinary way, was fitted in this dome. The so-called night periscope, a binocular instrument projecting a few inches above the top of the casing, gave some sort of a view when travelling on the surface in rough weather and large objects could be distinguished at a range of a few feet when submerged in daylight in clear water.

The purpose of the W & D was to allow one of the crew to leave and re-enter the X-craft when it was submerged. It was self-contained, with its own compensating tank and pump, and could be filled and emptied without altering the trim of the submarine. In it was the forehatch, used by a diver when cutting nets or clearing other obstructions. The only other hatch was in the control room.

There was no conning tower and the flat top of the casing was only a few inches above water when running on the surface. A hinged induction trunk could, however, be raised through which air was drawn when it was too rough to keep a hatch open.

The German bases were a long way from our own coasts so the midgets would have to be towed into position before beginning operations. A special slip for this purpose was fitted in the bow, controlled from inside the submarine. As the heavy ships were anchored many miles from the coast the midgets would still have to travel quite a long way on their own and the crew would be living on board, unsupported, for several days. In the crowded interior, space had to be found for stores, rudimentary cooking equipment and fresh water. There was a single folding bunk in the control room and room for a second man to stretch out on deck in the fore-end. There was, of course, all the usual equipment for navigating and controlling the submarine—magnetic and gyro compasses, an aircraft-type direction indicator, steering and hydroplane gear, trim and compensating pumps, high pressure air control valves, oxygen equipment and stowage for the underwater breathing apparatus or D.S.E.A.,* for use by a diver or for escaping in an emergency.

Volunteers from very fit men who were good swimmers had already been called for 'for special and hazardous service'. The first of them formed the original crew of X 3, Lieut. W. S. Meeks, D.S.C., R.N., Lieut. Donald Cameron R.N.R. and Chief E. R. A. Richardson. In the Spring of 1943 the first regular training classes began at Fort Blockhouse, and in August the Kyles of Bute Hydropathic Hotel on Loch Striven and a shooting-lodge at the head of the loch became H.M.S. *Varbel* for further training, using X 3 and her experimental sister X 4, whilst the operational X-craft, numbers 5, 6, 7, 8, 9 and 10, were being completed. Cameron was now in command of X 3 and Lieutenant B. C. G. Place R.N. of X 4.

The two principal actors in this story were both small men, tough and wiry. Don Cameron, twenty-six years old, was born at Carluke, Lanarkshire. He had originally

* Davis Submarine Escape Apparatus.

wished to join the R.A.F. and had passed into Cranwell before the war, only to be told he was too young to be accepted for another few months. Riled by the delay he joined the Merchant Navy. In September 1939 he was serving as midshipman R.N.R. in an armed merchant cruiser. Patrolling the North Atlantic was too slow for him so he volunteered for submarines in August 1940 and did a number of patrols in the North Sea and Channel in the *Sturgeon*. Tenacious, courageous and enterprising he was a natural choice for the first X-craft, where he soon showed that the confidence placed in his abilities had not been misdirected. At Gosport in 1940 he had met and married his wife Eve, who was serving in the W.R.N.S. Their first baby was born in 1942.

Godfrey Place, born in Little Malvern, Worcestershire was twenty-two. After spending much of his childhood in Northern Rhodesia and Uganda he joined the Navy as a cadet, and volunteered for submarines in 1941. He had served in the famous Malta submarine flotilla for some time, a very steady, reliable and thorough young officer who was awarded the D.S.C. in the *Unbeaten,* and the Polish Cross of Valour whilst acting as liaison officer with the *Sokol*.

He had a foretaste of the future when in Malta. After an evening on leave in Valletta he was returning to the submarine base at Fort Manoel on the opposite side of Sliema harbour. It was a long way round by road, so Place decided to swim across the creek. He was stark naked, his clothes done up in a neat bundle and tied on the top of his head, when he was arrested by a Maltese sentry, quite sure he had captured an Italian frogman and making very free with his fixed bayonet. 'You feel extremely un-protected in such circumstances', said Godfrey Place.

Returning to England in 1942 he 'found himself' (his own expression) a volunteer for X-craft. Whose ever choice it was, it was a good one and in the summer of 1943 he was helping Cameron to train the operational crews for the six new X-craft in Loch Striven.

There was much to learn and the training period was not without its difficulties, and tragedies. Whilst X 4 was exercising on the surface a wave washed Sub-Lieut. Morgan Thomas R.N.V.R. off the casing. The fore-hatch was open, the W & D was flooded and X 4, floating almost vertically in the water, was in a nasty predicament, with E.R.A. Whitley shut off in the fore-end and Place isolated in the engine room. Poor Thomas was drowned before help arrived. X 4 was towed inshore and the others rescued, but not for several hours. X 3, with a trainee crew commanded by Lieut. John Lorimer, was flooded and sunk when the induction valve jammed open. The three men aboard escaped by D.S.E.A. and X 3 was raised and put back into service. These accidents underlined the perils of the new venture.

It had been hoped to stage the operation against the German capital ships in March 1944 using only three X-craft, but the training took longer than expected. In February it was decided to postpone the attempt until September when all six boats would be available. The summer months, with their perpetual daylight (the most likely enemy anchorages were close to the Arctic Circle) were unsuitable. The delay was disappointing, but it was a fortunate decision, enabling training to proceed until both the X-craft and their crews were at concert pitch.

Training was exceedingly thorough. Aerial photographs revealed the German ships, lurking at the head of long fiords. The approaches to the fiords were mined, well patrolled by ships and aircraft and covered by guns on shore. There were anti-submarine nets across the mouths of the inner fiords and the ships themselves lay inside 'boxes' of anti-torpedo netting. These conditions were simulated in the lochs of the north-west coast of Scotland, using one of our own capital ships, the *Malaya*, as a target. There was now an advanced base for the midgets in Loch Cairnbawn (Port H.H.Z.). The X-craft would be towed to starting positions near Cape Wrath so that they must cover the appropriate distance before making their attacks.

Results were most encouraging, and often the midgets would bob up alongside without being detected. It was, however, found that the difficulties of passing nets were considerable. Movement of the supporting buoys on the surface would often betray X-craft trying to slip through anti-submarine nets; cutting the close mesh of anti-torpedo netting was almost impossible. Sub-Lieutenant David Locke R.N.V.R. was lost when exercising net-cutting from Place's X 7. Locke lost consciousness when he had been breathing oxygen for some time, but why this happened was, at that time, a mystery. After this accident a trained driver was added to the complement of each X-craft—making four in all, usually three officers and an Engine Room Artificer. The method of getting the X-craft into position, something like 1000 miles from Scotland to the starting point for solo work, was also perfected. Using conventional submarines as tugs, X-craft could be towed both on the surface and submerged. Surprise being the essence of the operation it was hoped by this means to take the enemy entirely unawares.

In July Godfrey Place was married to Second Officer Althea Tucker W.R.N.S. The difficulty of seeing something of his young wife was another problem which had to be tackled, and was occasionally overcome. But as the time drew nearer security precautions were increased and from 1 September no leave was given to anyone from Port H.H.Z.

Early in September the great battleship *Tirpitz* (42,500 tons), the battle-cruiser *Scharnhorst* and the pocket-battle-ship *Lützow* were all in the neighbourhood of Alten Fiord, just inside the Arctic Circle in North Norway. On 6 September *Tirpitz* and *Scharnhorst* disappeared. Next day they were off Spitzbergen with twelve destroyers and carried out a tip and run raid, chiefly directed against the coal mines. With the X-craft due to sail on 11 September it was important to keep track of their movements. Bad weather hid the fiords from observation until 10 September, when the welcome news was received that they were back in Alten Fiord, the *Tirpitz* in her nest of nets at the head of Kaa Fiord, the *Scharnhorst* similarly protected further down, with the *Lützow* in Lange Fiord nearby.

Aerial reconnaissance by the R.A.F. had already played a big part in the preparations and it was essential to have up-to-date information about the German ships during the long tow north. After a good deal of haggling the Russians had given permission for a flight of reconnaissance Spitfires to operate from Vaenga airfield, and it was hoped that Mosquitos, flying from Scotland to Murmansk, would be able to supplement the information they supplied. A shuttle service of Catalina flying boats between N. Russia and Scotland was laid on to bring home the photographs. The Russian C.-in-C., Northern Fleet seemed anxious to co-operate, but had to refer to Moscow. There were all sorts of bureaucratic delays, culminating in a threat to deny the use of Vaenga airfield, though the Russian airmen there did all they could to help. Matters climbed to what the British Admiral in N. Russia (Rear Admiral Archer) described as a 'high degree of fantasy' when customs officials impounded the life-saving carrier pigeons of the Catalinas on the ground that it was illegal to import livestock into the U.S.S.R. without a permit. But somehow the necessary sorties were flown, though the weather prevented the latest photographs being available when the six X-craft, in tow of six big submarines, sailed for Norway on 11 and 12 September. Admiral Sir Claud Barry, who had taken a keen personal interest in every detail, was there to see them off.

The journey to the slipping position would take eight days. The operational crews must be fit and fresh on arrival so they travelled 'soft' in the bigger submarines, the midgets being manned by passage crews, three men in each X-craft. The midgets were towed dived, surfacing three or four times every twenty-four hours to ventilate the boats. When dived, two men were on watch, steering

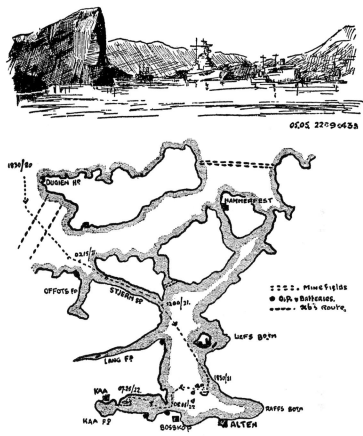

The attack on the *Tirpitz*. Taken from Donald Cameron's note-book, the upper sketch shows his periscope-view of the target just after five a.m. on 22 September 1943. The map is not to scale; the actual distance from the marked position of the X-craft at 02.15 on the 21st to that at noon on the same day is about seventeen miles, and the run from noon 21st to five a.m. 22nd a further twenty.

---

and controlling the trim, whilst the third got some rest. Quite a lot of routine maintenance had to be done and the cramped conditions made this long journey a considerable feat in itself. The contribution of the passage crews was unspectacular, but very real.

For the first three days the weather was good and

all went well, but on 15 September the wind got up, raising a nasty sea. At 4.0 a.m. X 8 parted her tow with the *Seanymph,* surfaced, hurried along alone and was eventually recovered, though not until late the following day. X 7 also parted her tow, but kept in contact with the *Stubborn* whilst the auxiliary tow was passed. On 16 September *Syrtis* gave the usual signal to X 9 to surface and ventilate, but the X-craft failed to appear. *Syrtis* turned back to search for X 9, but could not find her. The tow must have parted some time before. Had the weight of the tow-rope carried X 9 into the depths before she could correct her trim? The facts will never be known, for nothing more was heard of Sub-Lieutenant E. Kearon R.N.V.R. and his crew.

Next day X 8 was again in difficulties. The big side-charges had built-in buoyancy compartments to 'trim' them. These compartments were leaking in one of her charges. The defect had never been experienced during trials and the X-craft had no means of correcting a list except by shifting stores and other moveables. The charge had to be jettisoned, but the same defect developed in the other charge next day. This charge detonated after being jettisoned, the force of the explosion seriously damaging X 8 although she was three miles away. She was now incapable of diving and would compromise the operation if sighted on the surface. Her crew was taken off and she was scuttled.

These were serious set-backs, but the other four X-craft were still in good shape. The weather was improving and on the eighth day after leaving Port H.H.Z. the expedition sighted the tops of the Norwegian mountains, making a land-fall on time and where expected. By dawn on 20 September the operational crews had taken over. X 5, X 6 and X 7 had arrived in perfect condition and although X 10 had defects in the periscope hoist and wet and dry pump motors they were not regarded as serious. All the crews were fit and well and in excellent spirits. Although they had not seen the latest aerial reconnaissance photographs, a full description had been signalled during the passage north. Briefing about the anchorages had been so complete that no one anticipated any difficulties on this score.

X 7 was still in tow of *Stubborn* when she had a nasty experience. A mine caught across the tow-rope and slid down it on to the midget's bows. Place went up on to the casing, sat on the bow and succeeded in pushing it clear with his feet. Cameron found that the buoyancy chambers of his starboard charge were flooding, but managed to correct the list by shifting stores and spare gear over to port.

It had been intended that X 5, X 6 and X 7 should attack the *Tirpitz*, X 8 the *Lützow* and X 9 and X 10 the *Scharnhorst*. These targets were not altered. Exactly at the time and in the position planned the four remaining X-craft were slipped and sent off on their great adventure.

The orders for the operation included plans for picking up the X-craft on their return, three or four days later if everything went well—a big 'if'. The large submarines remained in the offing, ready to intercept any game flushed by their small consorts. At night they closed the coast, visiting various pre-arranged rendezvous. A week passed without any news, but on the eighth day *Stubborn* sighted X 10 in a fiord of Söröy Island and took her in tow.

Her commanding officer, Lieutenant Hudspeth had an interesting story to tell. He had penetrated almost to the mouth of the inner fiord where the *Scharnhorst* should have been lying, but had been forced to turn back by defects. Both compasses were out of action, the periscope could not be raised or lowered and there were other troubles. Reluctantly Hudspeth had abandoned the attempt and had spent the next six days hiding in various fiords. It was quite a little saga in itself, but what had happened to X 5, X 6 and X 7? Hudspeth had heard two very heavy explosions not long after 8.0 a.m. on 22 September, which was within the time fixed for the attack. Reconnaissance flights on September 23 revealed the *Tirpitz* in her usual position, but surrounded by great smears of oil fuel which trailed off down the fiord. But it was many months before the story of what had occurred was told.

From the slipping position to the entrance of Kaa Fiord was about fifty miles. The first obstacle to be negotiated was a minefield. This the X-craft crossed on the surface, on D day, 20 September. They were acting independently and were some distance apart. Don Cameron in X 6 sighted a patrol craft, but avoided her without difficulty. Darkness had fallen when they approached the entrance of the long, narrow channel between Stjernöy Island and the mainland. X 7 saw X 5 shortly before midnight. Place shouting 'good hunting and good luck' and Henty-Creer, who had been his best man at the wedding seven weeks before, returned the greeting.

Stjern Sund was to be negotiated submerged and be-tween 1.0 and 2.0 a.m. the X-craft dived and, now some distance apart, entered the sound. Trimming was difficult because the water was partly fresh; navigation in the dark was tricky, but less of a problem than had been feared. It was a dead calm night with the moon in its last quarter, just light enough for the loom of the land on either side to be distinguished. The very thorough briefing which the crews had received, with models, charts and photo-graphs now paid a dividend.

Cameron's periscope was fogging up, a defect which was to have serious consequences. Place sighted and avoided a number of vessels, but none of the X-craft was seen by the enemy. At first light, around 3.0 a.m., they were still in the Stjern Sund. A fine day dawned, with a nice ripple on the water. By noon they were in Alten Fiord, near the entrance to Lange Fiord, dodging an occasional A.S. patrol vessel and going deep whenever an aircraft appeared. At 4.30 p.m. Place saw a large warship near Aaroy Island which looked like the *Scharnhorst*,*

* It *was* the *Scharnhorst*, out for gunnery practice in Alten Fiord. If X 10 had got through she would have found the net-cage empty, for *Scharnhorst* did not return until 22 September.

178

but the *Tirpitz* was his target so he kept on. That evening both X 6 and X 7, though never sighting one another, were in their waiting positions amongst the group of islets centred on Brattholm, close to the entrance to Kaa Fiord. It had been hoped that the islets would give good cover, but they spent 'a rather disturbed night, charging, making good defects and dodging traffic'. Cameron stripped and dried out his periscope. He found that the clock on his port charge was defective, so set the fuse to fire one hour after release. X 7 had a leaky diesel exhaust pipe which filled the boat with fumes. It was an old trouble and Place carried a spare, but it did not fit. E.R.A. W. M. Whitley, lying flat in the very confined engine room, somehow managed to make a satisfactory joint with tape and chewing gum.

Long before first light Don Cameron got underway and headed for Kaa Fiord. X 7 had preceded him about an hour earlier, but this he did not know. As soon as he dived the periscope began to cloud over again, but he passed successfully through the gap in the boom at the entrance to the fiord, and had his first view of the great ship which had been the object of so much work and thought for the last eighteen months. It was 5.5 a.m.

The *Tirpitz* was lying with her bows pointing almost down the fiord, a magnificent ship with her wide beam, flaring bow and towering superstructure. Slightly nearer were two tankers, the smaller one anchored close inshore to port and the larger, a big vessel of the *Altmark* class, lying in the centre of the fiord. Some destroyers were secured alongside the big tanker and another was at anchor close by. The dark-green sea was glassy calm and all the ships were backed by the encircling hills, covered in brown scrub. Near the edge of the fiord was a narrow edging of bright green grass. Don Cameron estimated that the *Tirpitz* was just over a mile away.

But the periscope was clouding over badly. He dived to sixty feet and carried on by dead reckoning whilst the eyepiece was once more stripped and cleaned. This improved matters, but only slightly and when he again came to periscope depth he almost blundered into the anchored destroyer, just missing her stem. The big tanker was now between him and the *Tirpitz* so he swung to starboard to clear her, following the shore of the fiord. About half an hour later he was approaching the nets around the *Tirpitz*. A small coaster had been making up the fiord ahead of him, presumably bringing stores to the *Tirpitz*. Cameron followed the same course, slipping through the opened gate of the netted enclosure in her wake.

The enclosure was roughly the shape of the letter D, with the base facing the fiord. The *Tirpitz* was lying parallel to the long stroke and the shore formed the curved back. Cameron had planned to keep as near as he could to the shore, swing round and come under the battleship from her quarter. Half-blind as he was he ran aground and was forced to the surface. Reversing his motor he got off and under again, but the violent angles X 6 assumed in her struggles put the gyro compass out of action. With the periscope almost entirely useless Cameron made for the *Tirpitz*, luckily so large and so close that he could not miss her.

Godfrey Place in X 7 had left the waiting position an hour earlier than Cameron. He found the gap in the boom and started up Kaa Fiord, but was put deep by an outward bound motor launch. At 75 feet he ran into the edge of an empty net enclosure sometimes occupied by the *Lützow*.

It took about an hour to get clear, cautiously backing and filling and altering his trim. During these manoeuvres the boat took up some severe angles. The gyro-compass "toppled" and the compensating pump began to give trouble. At about 6.0 a.m. X 7 was again moving up the fiord, though finding it difficult to hold her trim at periscope depth. An hour later she was approaching the nets round the *Tirpitz*. Place went to 75 feet to pass below them.

The experts who had analysed the aerial photographs had decided that the double line of buoys were only large enough to support a net about 50 feet deep. The depth of the water was 120 feet so there should be plenty of space below them. One line of nets did, indeed, only extend 45 feet below the surface, but the second line, though formed of the same sized net, was suspended on jack-stays, overlapping the first line and hanging well below it. There was also a third line, invisible in the photographs, anchored to the bottom and kept upright by submerged buoys. The three lines formed a barrier from the surface to the bottom, though there were horizontal gaps between them. X 7, diving along at 75 feet passed below the first line, but was caught and held in the second.

Place went full astern and blew his ballast tanks. After a while X 7 came clear, but swung beam on to the net. She rose to the surface parallel to the line of buoys, but got under again unobserved. At 95 feet Place went ahead, turning towards the *Tirpitz*, only to be caught once more either by the second or third lines of nets.

'Here more difficulty in getting out was experienced,' wrote Place in his report, 'but after about 5 minutes of wriggling and blowing X 7 started to rise. The compass had, of course, gone wild on the previous surface and I was uncertain how close to the shore we were; so the motor was stopped and X 7 was allowed to come right up to the surface, with very little way on.'

'By some extraordinarily lucky chance', Place had passed through the nets. The *Tirpitz* was right ahead, and only thirty yards away. He ordered '40 feet. Full speed ahead' and was still going down when he struck the *Tirpitz* twenty feet below the waterline abreast 'B' turret and slid gently under her bottom, whose great expanse could be dimly seen through the clear, green water. Here 'in the full shadow of the ship', Place released his starboard charge.

X 7, with 60 feet showing on her diving gauges, had swung round and was now heading down the *Tirpitz's* keel, so Place caught a quick trim and went slowly ahead for about 150 or 200 feet under her bottom. When he estimated he was below 'X' turret he released his port charge. It was shortly after 7.30 a.m.

Life on board the great battleship had been following its normal routine. The hands had been called, the night defence crews and hydrophone listeners stood down, and the normal A/A and anti-sabotage watches set aboard and onshore. Around 7.15 a.m. a young seaman, on watch on deck, had spotted a long, black object close to the beach about 200 yards away. Nothing much ever seemed to happen in these ghastly northern solitudes; he was afraid of being laughed at if he started a scare, so he said nothing. It was probably a porpoise or some other out-landish beast. Five minutes later the object appeared again, in the middle of the netted enclosure and much closer. Several people now saw it. A submarine! The alarm was given, but the submarine had dived again. In any case she was far too close for the guns to be brought to bear. In something of a panic a boat was called away whilst the 2000 men on board the *Tirpitz,* boredom and frustration forgotten, rushed to their battle stations. Down below the engineers began frantically to raise steam and divers were told to get ready to go down to look for limpet mines.

After travelling for ten days and covering over 1000 miles X 6 and X 7 had arrived at their objective within a few minutes of one another. It was Cameron who had broken surface, eighty yards from the *Tirpitz,* abreast her bridge. He was quickly under again, moving towards her towering side, but a few minutes later he felt X 6 check as she met some obstruction. Thinking he had passed under her bottom and hit the nets on the other (starboard) side Cameron rose to the surface to see where he was. It was not the nets he had fouled, but something hanging down from some boats secured alongside the battleship. He was right under the great flare of her port bow. He manoeuvred X 6 until she was lying almost parallel with the *Tirpitz* and went astern until his propeller guard was scraping the cliff-like side. He now released both his side charges, depositing four tons of amatol right alongside abreast 'B' turret. Without a periscope X 6 had no chance of returning to the open sea, so the inboard vents were opened to scuttle her. Cameron and his crew climbed out, stepping into a German boat without even getting their feet wet. The boat tried to take X 6 in tow, but she was sinking fast and soon disappeared to join her charges on the bottom. Cameron, Lorimer, Kendall and Goddard were taken aboard the *Tirpitz*.

Meanwhile Place, in X 7, his charges safely laid, had gone to 100 feet and turned in the direction which he hoped would bring him to the spot where he had passed in through the net. His gyro-compass was still wild. At 60 feet he was in the net again.

'I had no exact idea of where we were; the difficulties we had experienced and the air trimmings had used two air bottles and only 1200 lbs., were left in the third. X 7's charges were due to explode in an hour—not to mention others which might go up any time after 0800.'

For a quarter of an hour Place struggled to get free, going full ahead to push the net as far as possible one way whilst blowing economically (air was running short) and then reversing his motor so as to get as much way on the boat as the slack of the nets would allow. Eventually the impetus given to X 7 by this means tore her clear. She came out of the net and slid over the head rope between the buoys on the surface. It was 7.40 a.m., about five minutes after X 6's crew had been taken aboard the *Tirpitz*.

The Germans now sighted X 7 for the first time. She was just off the battleship's port bow, too close for any large gun to be brought to bear, but a hot fire was opened on her with automatic weapons. Bullets could be heard hitting the casing as she slid under again.

The presence of a second submarine, apparently outside the nets, caused a considerable stir. How many others might there be? The Captain of the *Tirpitz,* deciding that he was safest inside the enclosure, gave up his plan of putting to sea, but ordered the ship to be moved as far as possible from the spot where X 6 had scuttled herself. The battleship's stern was secured by wires to the shore, but her bow was held by two anchors laid some distance apart. By hauling in on the starboard cable and veering the port the great ship's bow was swung slowly to starboard.

The Germans were, not unnaturally, in an excited state. The crews of midget submarines would never pass muster in Savile Row and the four prisoners from X 6, unshaven and dirty, were a disreputable-looking lot. They had been taken below and given schnapps and hot coffee, but now it looked as if they might be shot forthwith as saboteurs. Fortunately calmer counsels prevailed, but Don Cameron and his men, knowing they were sitting over at least four tons of amatol, were not entirely reassured. Their charges had been set for 8.0 a.m. and it was now after 7.45 a.m.

X 7 was sitting on the bottom just outside the nets, running her air compressor to replenish her exhausted supplies of air for blowing the tanks. The compasses were still out of action so Place now tried to come to periscope depth so that he could see which way X 7 was pointing. He could then start the direction indicator and set a course down the fiord. He was still 60 feet below the surface when he blundered back into the nets, this time on the starboard of the *Tirpitz* though Place by now had lost all sense of direction and had no idea where he was. He was struggling to free himself when, at 8.12 a.m., the first of the charges went off, detonating the other three.

The X-craft though small were extremely tough. Eight tons of amatol exploding within a few hundred feet of

X 7 shook her very violently, but did not destroy her. She was catapulted out of the net and shot to the surface where it was 'tiresome to see the *Tirpitz* still afloat'. Place went to the bottom again to survey the damage to his submarine.

It was, in the circumstances, surprisingly light. The after hatch was leaking, but the pressure hull was intact. Both compasses and all the diving gauges were out of action, but the other machinery was functioning. Place decided to come up, but as soon as he left the bottom he was in difficulties. The boat was not answering properly to her controls and could not be trimmed level, and the water which had leaked through the hatch, cascading forward and aft, accentuated the trouble. Several times X 7 broke surface, to be greeted by an accurate fire. Hits could be heard on the casing and the hull, aggravating the damage and making it more difficult than ever to hold a trim. Place struggled on, painfully covering a few hundred yards of the fifty mile journey to the open sea. Clearly he could never reach safety. He would have to abandon ship and scuttle his X-craft.

Patrols had been dropping depth-charges which had done no further damage to X 7, but which would be fatal to men using their D.S.E.A. He decided to surface before abandoning ship. Up he came. to be greeted by another hail of fire. The hatch was opened and Place climbed on to the casing, stripped off his white sweater and began to wave it. They had surfaced alongside a battle-practice target anchored in the fiord. Although all the ballast tanks had been blown some of them had been holed and were not empty. X 7 was very low in the water. She began to go down again and the hatch had to be closed. Place jumped on to the target as she disappeared.

The Germans had ceased fire. A boat approached, picked him up and took him at once to the *Tirpitz*. Trouserless, clad only in a vest, long submarine pants and a pair of flying boots he was an odd sight standing under the guns of 'Y' turret on the quarterdeck amongst his smartly uniformed captors. As he was being interrogated the guns suddenly began to fire again.

A *third* submarine had been reported, four or five hundred yards away outside the nets.

It was Henty Creer in X 5. After a few minutes the firing ceased, the guns crews claiming that they had scored direct hits. To make sure, patrols rushed up and plastered the spot where she had disappeared with depth-charges. The Germans had, alas, been all too successful and nothing further was ever heard of gallant X 5.

But three men remained alive in X 7. She had plunged to the bottom, but the hull was still tight. Whittam, Aitken and Whitley decided to use their D.S.E.A. sets, in which they had full confidence, to escape. As only one man could go out through the W & D, whose hatch could not be closed after him from inside, they decided to flood the boat, and then use both hatches. Some of the inboard vents had jambed and this took a long time. The water was very cold, and when its level reached the electric circuits the lights went out and the unflooded space filled with fumes. They put on their sets and started to breathe oxygen. Not much was known in 1943 about the dangerous effects of breathing oxygen under pressure (60 lbs per square inch at 20 fathoms). Sub-Lieut. Aitken just managed to hold out until the flooding had equalised the pressure, allowing the hatches to be opened, but Lieut. L. B. Whittam R.N.V.R. and E.R.A. W. M. Whitley died before they could escape. Aitken was picked up on the surface at 11.15 a.m. and brought to join the other five on board the *Tirpitz*.

Tirpitz, though still afloat, was seriously damaged. X 6's two charges and X 7's first charge had been close to her side when they went off and X 7's second charge under the engine rooms. The great ship had lifted bodily for several feet, throwing men off their feet and causing a number of casualties. The lights went out. In the darkness fittings torn from the bulkheads crashed to the deck. When the ship had ceased to whip and quiver she began to list to port. Order was gradually restored and the heel corrected.

Two of her four 15-inch turrets, each weighing some 2000 tons, had leapt off their roller bearings and could not be trained. All three sets of main engines were out of action. Damage to range-finders, communications, and to the sensitive gunnery control equipment was extensive. There was 500 tons of water in various flooded compartments. Casualties were small—1 killed and 40 wounded, but *Tirpitz*, 1500 miles from the nearest dockyard and unable to move under her own power, was crippled. It was six months before she was ready for sea again.

After being well treated on board the *Tirpitz* the six survivors started next day on the long journey to prison camps in Germany. Several months elapsed before anxious relatives in Britain knew which of the twelve very brave men who had penetrated Kaa Fiord were still alive. Lorimer, Kendall and Aitken were decorated with the D.S.O., Goddard received the C.G.M. and the two commanding officers, Cameron and Place were awarded the Victoria Cross. None of our honours and awards except the V.C. can be awarded posthumously, but the Submarine Service does not forget those who died on this great adventure—Whittam and Whitley; Henty-Creer, Nelson, Malcolm and Mortiboys.

I began this chapter by telling how Admiral Sir Max Horton put the wheels in motion which produced the little X-craft which, in the words of an American naval officer had 'got themselves a battleship for breakfast'. The closing words of his signal of congratulation to the Twelfth Submarine Flotilla are a fitting finale.

'The long approach voyage in unparalleled conditions, culminating in the successful attack on the target, called for and produced the highest degree of endurance and seamanlike skill.

'While deploring with you the loss of officers and men whose gallantry is unsurpassed in the history of the Submarine Service, I rejoice at the success which crowned this magnificent feat of arms.'

CHAPTER TWELVE

FRASER AND MAGENNIS

AT the end of 1944 the Navy, its commitments greatly reduced in the Atlantic, Mediterranean and Home waters, was preparing to send a strong force to the Far East. The British Pacific Fleet under the command of Admiral Sir Bruce Fraser was to include aircraft carriers, battleships, cruisers, destroyers and submarines. One of the submarine flotillas, the Fourteenth, would consist of six X-craft with their depot ship, H.M.S. *Bonaventure*. Captain W. R. (Tiny) Fell, D.S.O., Royal Navy, was in command.

The midget submarines were generally similar to those used for the attack on the *Tirpitz*, but 'tropicalised'. In a temperate climate, surrounded by cold water, life on board a midget had been strenuous and uncomfortable. With the sea temperature in the eighties and even higher air temperatures it would have been intolerable. Experience in larger submarines had proved that humidity is a worse enemy than heat. The XE-craft, as they were called, were fitted with a ventilating system and a small refrigerating plant which would slightly cool the air and, more important, keep the humidity down by extracting moisture. It had the additional advantages of providing ample supplies of fresh water for drinking, cooking and even washing. There was a small domestic refrigerator for food and drink. An apparatus for extracting CO_2 from the air and adding oxygen had also been installed.

The XE's, built in 1944 by Vickers-Armstrongs Ltd. at Barrow-in-Furness, had other modifications dictated by experience. The side-cargoes had been enlarged and a single one could now carry a charge of four tons of amatol.

An alternative type of side cargo had been developed which was really a container for limpet mines—small mines fitted with magnets which would hold them on a ship's bottom. Limpet mines had to be placed by hand. To facilitate this operation the XE-craft had folding antennae forward and aft which could be raised vertically above the casing, so that a midget with slight positive buoyancy would float a few feet below the flat bottom of a ship, (like a table upside-down), whilst the diver did his work. Another important improvement was a very accurate echo-sounding machine, with a dial in the control room showing the exact depth of water under the keel.

The weapon was ready, but there was a long period of frustration before it could be tried out against the enemy. In February 1945 *Bonaventure* carrying XE 1-6 sailed for Australia via the Panama Canal. The fact that midget submarines were being sent to the Pacific was 'Top Secret', and no shore leave was allowed when she called at Trinidad and San Diego. This restriction was particularly exasperating at the Californian port where the young men cooped up on board could see many highly delectable American girls just across the water and had to refuse, with the most genuine regret, invitations to visit Hollywood and other Elysian spots. In Pearl Harbour leave was at last given and the British sailors were royally entertained, but Captain Fell learnt to his dismay that the American Commander-in-Chief, Admiral Chester Nimitz, was opposed to the use of X-craft in the Pacific. *Bonaventure* arrived in Australia wondering if her long journey had been really necessary.

It was not until July 1945 that the tide of bad luck which seemed to be sweeping the Fourteenth Flotilla to oblivion changed, when Admiral James Fife U.S.N., the senior submarine officer in the Pacific, agreed to use the XE-craft for two operations which they alone could attempt—cutting the telegraph cables between Singapore and Tokio where they lay in shallow water off Hong Kong and Saigong, and attacking two heavy Japanese cruisers anchored off Singapore Dockyard. The curtain-raiser had been long and dull, but now at last the play was about to commence. This story deals with the attack on the cruisers, for which XE 1 (Lieutenant J. E. Smart M.B.E., R.N.V.R.) and XE 3 (Lieutenant I. E. Fraser D.S.C., R.N.R.) were selected.

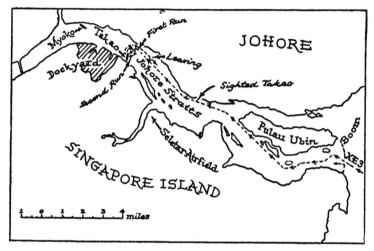

Johore Strait.

The operation, bearing the rather sinister name of 'Struggle', was planned to follow much the same pattern as the attack on the *Tirpitz* though the conditions were somewhat different. XE 1 and XE 3 would be towed by the conventional submarines *Spark* and *Stygian* from Labuan Island off north-west Borneo to the entrance of the Singapore Strait, about 650 miles. From the slipping position it was a further forty miles to Singapore Dockyard.

Singapore Island, almost on the equator (1°20′N.Lat.) is close to the tip of the Malay peninsular. It is about the size and shape of the Isle of Wight with the city of Singapore on its southern extremity. Ten miles to the north the Dockyard faces the mainland across the narrow dividing strait, spanned by an artificial causeway. This causeway is west of the Dockyard. The ship-channel follows the Johore Strait, a waterway twelve miles long skirting the north-east coast of Singapore Island. The strait is a mile to a mile and a quarter wide in its upper reaches, but narrower lower down where it divides into two arms around the island of Palau Ubin. The northern arm, known as Nana's Channel, was believed to be effectively blocked. The only entrance was between the eastern extremities of Singapore Island and Palau Ubin —a channel one-third of a mile wide, which was closed by a boom.

The *Myoko* was lying near the causeway and the *Takao* a short way east of the Dockyard. Neither ship, heavy cruisers of 13,400 tons armed with ten 8-inch and eight 5.1-inch guns and 16 torpedo tubes, was surrounded by nets, but they were anchored close to the shore in very shallow water and were partly aground at low tide. They had not been to sea for some time, but their powerful gun armament was an important addition to the defences of the base.

On 26 July the little expedition left the tropical paradise of Labuan. The passage, with the towing submarines dived by day and on the surface at night, was uneventful. At 6.0 a.m., on 30 July, in the blackness of the tropical night, the operational crews took the place of the passage crews, paddling across the dead-calm sea in rubber dinghies. All four submarines submerged and continued their journey with the midgets still in tow. When darkness had again fallen they surfaced a few miles from the Horsburgh Light, which had not been extinguished by the enemy. Just after 11.0 p.m. the tows were released and the little XE-craft went on alone, skirting the southern end of the Johore peninsula. *Spark* and *Stygian* waited outside the eastern entrance of the Singapore Strait, hoping to pick up their small charges about forty-eight hours later. XE 1, whose target was the *Myoko*, was in the lead, about six miles ahead of XE 3.

With Fraser in XE 3 were his First Lieutenant, Sub-Lieutenant W. J. L. Smith R.N.Z.N.V.R., Engine Room Artificer C. A. Reed and Acting Leading Seaman J. J. Magennis, the last two regular naval ratings. The passage crew under Sub-Lieutenant Frank Ogden R.N.V.R. had done their arduous job splendidly and XE 3 was in apple-pie order, a wonderful tribute to the men who had spent four days working and sweating in a hot-house atmosphere and a very confined space, with very little rest and without the incentive of action to follow. They had rectified all the small defects which had occurred and kept the boat clean and dry whilst competing with the problem of being towed for long hours at speeds up to eleven knots.

The most experienced midget submariner in XE 3's crew was 'Mick' Magennis, the diver, who had been one of X 7's passage crew in the *Tirpitz* operation. Magennis, born in Belfast with a Scottish father and an Irish mother was a little man, full of energy and pluck. He had joined the Navy as a boy, but had not found peacetime sailoring much to his liking. It was better when the war came along and he had quite enjoyed himself in the destroyer *Kandahar* until she was sunk off Tripoli in December 1941. He was by temperament a small ship man, independent and impatient of 'spit and polish' discipline. He volunteered for submarines in 1942, spent some time in the larger boats and found his true vocation when he transferred to X-craft. He had always been fond of swimming and took naturally to his new job as a diver. The crew of an X-craft must be very closely knit and commanding officers were allowed as far as possible to pick their own men. Magennis had been with Fraser in XE 3 from the beginning. He was twenty-five years old.

'Tich' Fraser, 5 feet 4 inches tall, was an even smaller man than Magennis and two years his junior. He too had gone to sea as a lad, joining the training ship *Conway* at fifteen and later serving in the Merchant Navy with the Blue Star Line. Fraser wanted to get into the Navy, and it had been a bitter blow when he failed the entrance examination. He joined the Royal Naval Reserve and was doing his four months' training as a Midshipman R.N.R. in a destroyer when war broke out. After serving in various destroyers until 1941 he volunteered for submarines 'for no valid reason which I can now recall' and was third officer in the *Sahib,* in the Tenth (Malta) Submarine Flotilla in 1942. *Sahib* distinguished herself, sinking U 301 and a number of supply ships and Fraser was awarded the D.S.C. At an hilarious party following a successful patrol someone dropped a heavy brass ashtray on his foot, and Fraser was in hospital when *Sahib* was sunk and her crew taken prisoner. On his return to England he married his boyhood sweetheart, Miss Melba Hughes then serving in the W.R.N.S. Appointed First Lieutenant of an old H class submarine doing useful but monotonous duty as a target for A.S. vessels under training, Fraser volunteered for 'special and hazardous service' and in 1944 was with the X-craft training in Loch Striven. When XE 3 was nearing completion he went to Barrow to take her over. A period of 'working-up' followed around the north-west coast of Scotland. Fraser seemed to take it all very lightly, but he was an excellent seaman and very much more thorough and conscientious than he would have you believe. He also used his head. In a dummy attack on the *Bonaventure* he baffled the listening posts by drifting into her anchorage on the flood tide; holding a perfect trim, but dispensing altogether with his main motor. On another occasion he was able to locate the carefully hidden *Bonaventure* with surprising ease by following his hunch that the captain, a keen trout fisherman, would probably be lurking in a place giving the best opportunities for his sport.

E. R. A. Reed, quiet, cheerful and extremely competent was another 'founder-member' of the crew, but 'Kiwi' Smith had only joined a few weeks before when the original First Lieutenant, Sub-Lieutenant David Carey had been lost, from causes not fully explained, but probably from oxygen poisoning, when XE 3 was practising cable-cutting off the Australian coast. Smith was, however, an experienced X-craft hand.

After negotiating the Singapore Strait in the darkness Fraser planned to be off the entrance of Johore Strait just before dawn. As soon as it was light enough to see through the periscope he would approach the boom. It was improbable that they would be lucky enough to find the gate open, and a certain amount of daylight was necessary if Magennis, issuing from the Wet and Dry, was to cut a hole through the net for XE 3.

At 11.0 p.m. *Stygian* vanished in the darkness astern. She had brought XE 3 rather farther than expected before slipping the tow, so Fraser believed he had a little time in hand if the tide, which was flowing against him, was as shown on the chart. On the surface, using her diesel engine, XE 3 slid along at five knots, skirting the black shape of the low-lying coast. The moon had not yet risen and it was very dark. Fraser stood on the casing, continually sweeping the sea around him through his glasses. Below only the red lights which gave just enough illumination for the various instruments and controls were burning. Reed was at the steering wheel at the forward end of the tiny control room. Behind him sat Smith at the operating position of the hydroplanes with the diving and trimming controls ready to hand. On the little table above the bunk, sections cut from the chart were spread. Fraser had memorised their particulars so thoroughly that he knew by heart the various courses to be steered. Daylight would come at about 7.30 a.m.*

There was a swept channel down the middle of the Singapore Strait, through the minefields laid by the British, Dutch and Japanese, but Fraser had decided to cut the corner to the entrance of Johore Strait, relying on the shallow draft of a surfaced X-craft to keep him out of trouble. The sea was completely calm, with no swell and without a ripple on its surface and XE 3, with her ballast tanks partly flooded, was trimmed right down. If

* The times used are those being kept in XE 3.

any small enemy craft were patrolling above the minefield the low silhouette would be very difficult to see, but tropical waters are highly phosphorescent and the bow wave splashing by and the wake stretching away astern seemed to Fraser to be very conspicuous indeed. Nothing could be done about this unpleasant phenomenon.

Intelligence had optimistically opined that he would find the various channel buoys lit, but there was no sign of them. Fortunately the night, though dark, was absolutely clear and he was able to fix his position, though not very accurately, by taking bearings of the low hills of Johore on his starboard hand and the edges of promontories. About two and a half hours after slipping he estimated that he was approaching the listening posts for submarines which were said to be located off south Johore. The diesel engine was stopped and XE 3 moved silently forward on her motor at reduced speed. For half an hour she crept along, but seemed to be making very little progress. Listening posts or no listening posts, this would not do, so Fraser re-started his diesel engine.

Except for the subdued rumble from below and the splashing of the bow wave it was extraordinarily quiet. Fraser was using the partly raised induction trunk as a voice-pipe to pass his orders to the control room, but Smith and Reed, with the little engine buzzing round close at hand, could not hear him unless he shouted. Sounds carry for a long way over the water and Fraser was fearful of attracting attention. He also found it difficult accurately to describe to Smith, following their progress on the chart, the features of which he was taking bearings. So he now opened the hatch. For the rest of the night he sat on the casing, with his legs dangling down the W & D, and occasionally slipping below to use the chart—a lesser risk than faulty navigation.

The time seemed to pass very slowly. It was peaceful up there in the warm tropic night. Spicey, indescribable scents wafted out from the sleeping land. The errand they were bound on seemed fantastic. Four men in a tiny submarine, heading steadily towards the lion's mouth, and very much alone. But at this moment everything, even the war, seemed insubstantial and far away. It would be teatime on the other side of the world where the summer sun might be shining. Peace had come to Europe. For many, the majority indeed, life was beginning to assume a more normal aspect. It was peaceful enough here, but what of the morrow? Fraser and his crew were all young men. Risks, which would have taken a great deal of facing up to a year before, assumed a pretty formidable shape in the small hours before dawn, when life is in any case said to be at its lowest ebb.

The moon was coming up and the sky getting brighter. Shortly after 3.0 a.m. Fraser spotted a shape ahead. One of the channel buoys: unlit, but it would give him an accurate fix. He altered course to pass close enough to distinguish its markings. Suddenly the "buoy" changed into the sail of a small fishing boat. Fraser hurriedly turned away. It was a shock to find how difficult objects were to distinguish even in the moonlight. An hour or so later two much larger objects loomed up ahead. Fraser decided they were a tanker and an escorting motor launch. They were coming his way and seemed to be approaching rather fast, so Fraser gave the order to dive and dropped below, arriving in the control room as XE 3 slid under water. The bottom was close and they hit it fairly hard, damaging the patent log. The loss of this very useful piece of equipment was quite serious as the exact distance run must now be calculated more laboriously and rather less accurately from the revolutions of the propeller shaft.

There was no sound of approaching ships so, after waiting for half an hour, Fraser cautiously rose to periscope depth. The two vessels were still in sight. Not liking to risk coming to the surface Fraser continued on his way submerged.

At this point everyone was suffering from the effects of twenty-four strenuous hours without proper sleep. They had rested a little during the previous day, but now it was almost impossible to keep awake. It was hot and very stuffy inside the submarine; there was no room to move about and they were nodding at their posts. This danger had been foreseen and benzedrine tablets were issued. There was no sign of the boom in the darkness, but it must be close at hand. Believing he was still ahead of time Fraser decided to go to the bottom for a while, to rest his crew and allow the benzedrine to take effect. For three quarters of an hour it was absolutely quiet in XE 3 except for the gentle hissing of the oxygen cylinder. Although no one slept for more than a few minutes, except Magennis who had somehow managed to stow his small body comfortably beside the engine, they were greatly refreshed when the time came to get under way. 'Morale was up 100 per cent', wrote Fraser later.

The boost was needed, for a disappointment was in store. At 7.45 a.m. Fraser rose to periscope depth. It was daylight, but the coasts of Singapore Island and Palau Ubin Island which flank the ends of the Strait were not in sight. Fraser rose until the casing was awash and eventually saw the land, but a long way off. The current must have been a great deal stronger than expected for a fix showed that they still had three and a half miles to cover before reaching the boom.

The boom would have to be passed in broad daylight, and he would need to hurry to reach the *Takao* before the falling tide put her hard aground. At this time, although he could not know it, the result of the whole operation was in the balance; for XE 1, which should have been well ahead of XE 3, was now astern of her. Smart had encountered a number of ships during the night which had delayed him seriously, and with even further to go to reach the *Myoko*, his chances of success were negligible.

But Fraser now had a stroke of luck. The gate in the boom was open. At 10.30 a.m. XE 3 slipped through, passing close to the rusty trawler which acted as a boom vessel. The sea was glassy calm and the pale green water as clear as crystal. At slow speed XE 3 crept along, using her periscope with extreme caution. There was no sign she had been either seen or heard as she finally entered Johore Strait.

There was still eleven miles to cover, which would take about three and a half hours. High tide was at noon. It would be after two o'clock before they made their attack. Luckily the rise and fall was not great, only about eight feet. There might be enough water, but they must hurry.

For three hours Fraser carefully made his way up the Straits. Bends in the channel limited the distance he could see ahead. To port was Singapore Island, covered in dark scrub and topped by low hills. After skirting the long shore of Pulau Ubin, the low, marshy coast of Johore came into view, shimmering in the heat-haze. There was not much traffic about and he was able to keep well clear of the ships he saw. The clear, green water through which XE 3 swam along was luke-warm. It was very hot inside the X-craft and all four men were streaming with sweat. Magennis gasped for breath as he struggled into his rubber diving dress—a difficult job at the best of times.

The ebb tide was against them and progress seemed very slow, but at noon they were more than half way up the Straits with the Buloh buoy abeam. XE 3 was nearing the point where the long reach off the Dockyard gradually opens up ahead. When Fraser put up his periscope at 12.50 p.m. he had his first view of the *Takao*.

As expected she was moored very close to Singapore Island with her bows pointing across the Straits to Johore. From XE 3 she was beam-on, with the open waters of the Reach behind her. Though still over three miles away the silhouette he had so often memorised was clearly visible.

There was no mistaking it. At last the target was in sight. Fraser called each man to the periscope in turn for a brief look.

For the next hour he kept close to the northern side

of the Strait, skirting the coast of Johore. When the *Takao* was almost abeam, and about a mile away, XE 3 was fine on her starboard bow.

In the very shallow water in which she was lying the *Takao* was almost aground except at the top of the tide. Now both her bow and stern would be nearly on the bottom, but the chart showed a deeper patch under her amidships. This patch was Fraser's objective, but to reach it he must cross the shallows which extended for some distance from the cruiser's bow. The shortest route was the one he had always planned to use, directly across the Straits. At 2.08 p.m. he turned to port and started his attack.

Fraser himself was at the periscope. Magennis, ready in his diving suit except for the headpiece, was beside him, noting bearings and using the slide-rule which converted periscope readings into ranges. Reed was steering. Smith controlled the hydroplanes and the trim pump. All four men, weariness forgotten, heat forgotten, fear forgotten, keyed up by the intense excitement of the moment, were quietly and efficiently carrying out the functions they had so often practised.

The *Takao* had been camouflaged to blend with the land behind her and although now so close was quite difficult to see. To starboard was the anchorage off the Dockyard. There were no heavy ships at the mooring buoys and the only warship visible was a destroyer escort. Several small boats were under way and a large merchant ship was anchored in the stream. The sea was absolutely calm and the water seemed alarmingly clear. Through the night periscope much of XE 3 was visible as she swam along.

Using the attacking periscope as little as possible Fraser approached the cruiser. After a longish period 'blind' he found himself very close to a motor-cutter, so close that every detail of the boat and the men on board could be distinguished. The boat was crowded with Japanese sailors, apparently going ashore on leave and perfectly oblivious of his presence. The periscope was hurriedly lowered as Fraser ordered Smith to go deep. With 30 feet showing on the gauge XE 3 grounded gently on the bottom.

The *Takao* had only been about 400 yards away and this must be the beginning of the shallow patch. Still forging slowly ahead XE 3 slid gradually up to 15 feet. At this depth the surface was only some ten feet above the casing. Fraser saw it as 'a wrinkled window-pane' of brightness above the clear green water. XE 3 was still close below the surface when she hit something solid and stopped. It was the *Takao*.

They had arrived, but not under her bottom as planned. XE 3 was lying parallel to the cruiser, bow to stern. Clearly she had hit well forward where the *Takao* was almost aground. A near-miss, but a miss nevertheless.

Fraser could have dropped his side charge at this point, but the thought seems never to have occurred to him. Instead he instantly decided to return to mid-channel and start again. He ordered hard a port and half ahead, intending to turn through 180 degrees. But at first XE 3 refused to move. It took about five minutes' careful manoeuvring before she came clear, swung towards the middle of the Strait, slid back over the shallows and was again in deep water. It was 3.3 p.m., almost an hour after he had begun his first attack, when Fraser was ready to try again. This time he altered his point of aim, making for the forward funnel of the *Takao*.

Leaving the deep water channel he hit an even shallower patch on the intervening bank which brought him up to thirteen feet. But as he anxiously watched the gauge the pointer began to swing clockwise again. He was sliding into deeper water. With twenty-four feet on the gauge the bright surface above suddenly went dark. XE 3 came gently to rest right under the *Takao's* bottom.

It was about a quarter past three, three hours after high water. The tide had dropped and the *Takao's* keel was very close to the top of the casing. From the keel

her bottom sloped upwards, more steeply than in com-
parable British ships. Long fronds of weed covered the
steel plating. Fraser ordered the forward antennae to be
raised but noted that they did not reach the dark green
surface above. It was not quite as he expected, but it
would have to do. Magennis was already in the W & D. In
a moment or two Fraser, watching through the night periscope, saw the hatch beginning to open. But above the
W & D *Takao's* sloping bottom was too close. The hatch
would not swing right back. If Magennis had not been a
small man and very determined, he could not have forced
himself through the narrow space. Fraser watched
anxiously as the diver struggled to get out, and was very
relieved when he emerged and floated fish-like away in
search of his limpet mines. There was a small leak from
the reducing valve of his oxygen mask from which a
stream of bright bubbles rose.

For nearly half an hour the three men inside the X-craft
waited as Magennis worked on. From the night periscope
it was as though XE 3 was lying in an underwater cave,
its roof the weed-covered bottom of the cruiser, its sides
the dim recesses beneath her, with bright water from the
sunlit world outside ahead. At intervals Magennis would
slide into view, carrying a limpet mine or vanishing over
the side in search of another one. It was stiflingly hot
inside the submarine and the time seemed to pass exceedingly slowly. Magennis was, in fact, having great difficulty
in fixing the limpets. Even when he had cut away the
weed with his knife the cruiser's bottom was encrusted
with barnacles and the magnets would not hold. It was
only by tying them in bunches of three, grouped on either
side of the keel that he could make them remain in place.
He worked on steadily, methodically, maddeningly un-
hurried. Fraser, Smith and Reed sweated and waited. Not
until 4.0 p.m. was the last of the limpets placed. Magennis
forced himself back into the W & D and closed the hatch.
Fraser could now give the order to release both side
cargoes, the four tons of amatol with its clock set for 9.30

p.m., and the empty limpet container. Soon now they could be on their way.

So far all the mechanical fittings of XE 3 had worked perfectly. The port side cargo fell away correctly, but the empty limpet container refused obstinately to swing clear. After struggling with it for a while Fraser, aware of the dropping tide and fearful of being trapped under the cruiser, tried to go ahead. XE 3 refused to budge. *Takao's* keel, resting on the casing behind the periscope standards prevented her going astern and at first she would not move ahead. Eventually she began to slide very slowly out into the sunlight, emerging on the *Takao's* port side. But the limpet container was still in place, half on and half off its stops, upsetting the trim and like a broken wing pulling XE 3 round to starboard. Fraser stopped his motor, sinking gently to the bottom about thirty feet from the cruiser's side. In that clear water anyone looking down from above could surely see the dark shape of the X-craft, lying less than twenty-five feet down.

Fraser considered what to do. The limpet container must be got clear, and only a diver could do it. Magennis, after his efforts with the mines, was exhausted. The only other man with sufficient diving experience was Fraser himself. If, as seemed very likely, they were seen, explosive charges would immediately be dropped. XE 3 might survive, but the diver would certainly be killed, leaving the others without the man most competent to navigate during the long return journey. It was an exceedingly difficult decision for Fraser. He had decided to go out himself when Magennis, now beginning to get his wind, begged to be allowed to make the attempt. Reluctantly Fraser agreed. After resting for a few more minutes Magennis, armed with a large spanner, re-entered the W & D. Fraser watched the hatch swing back, releasing a cloud of bubbles. Magennis floated out, spanner in hand, and disappeared over the side.

He seemed to be gone for a very long time. For the men inside, powerless to help and convinced that at any moment XE 3 would surely be seen, the delay was endless. Sometimes they could hear Magennis working away at the container. Then, for long minutes, there would be absolute silence, except for their own breathing and the hiss of the oxygen cylinder. It was a quarter of an hour, 4.40 p.m. and an hour and a half after they had started the first run in, before Magennis was back in the W & D. At full speed XE 3 slid out across the bank and turned down the Straits towards the open sea.

They had a long way to go and their troubles were not over. Patches of fresher water kept upsetting the trim. When only about a mile from the *Takao* they broke surface. The seconds which passed before they got under again seemed like hours. Off Serangoon a high-speed motor boat roared directly overhead and everyone waited for the crash of depth-charges, but she had not seen them. It was over three hours after they had left the *Takao* before they reached and safely passed the boom, nine hours and twenty minutes after entering the Straits. Reaction had set in and they were all deadly tired. Smith and Reed had scarcely moved from their posts for twelve hours and were stiff and cramped. Daylight lingered on. It was 9.0 p.m. before Fraser decided he could risk coming to the surface. It was now pitch dark and nothing could be seen through the periscope. There was no sound of propellers and the coast seemed to be clear. Fraser had a nasty scare when he found he had surfaced alongside a big junk, so close that he could hear the creak and rattle of her rigging as she rolled lazily in the swell.

The charges had been set to go off at 9.30 p.m. At 9.38 p.m. there was a flare of flame astern, beyond Singapore Island. Fraser called his little crew on deck one by one to watch the conflagration, a great pillar of flame and smoke towering into the sky.*

* The conflagration was not, in fact, caused by the X-craft charges. By an extraordinary coincidence an aircraft crashed on Singapore Island near to the Dockyard at this time. XE 3's charges exploded, tearing a great hole in the *Takao*'s bottom, but the ship did not catch fire.

But even this sight could hardly keep them awake. They were dropping with weariness. Fraser lashed himself to the induction trunk, for he kept on nodding off. For two more hours XE 3 rumbled steadily seaward. The welcome flash of Horsburgh light came up on the starboard bow. A quarter of an hour later a green light appeared ahead. It was the *Stygian*.

XE 1 also returned safely. Too late through the boom to reach the *Myoko* she had eventually penetrated as far as the *Takao* and dropped her charge alongside. For this exploit Lieutenant Smart was decorated the D.S.O. Fraser and Magennis were awarded the Victoria Cross, Smith received the D.S.O. and Reed the C.G.M.

EPILOGUE

Eleven of the officers and ratings about whom this book was written survived the two wars, though Lieutenant R. D. Sandford died in 1918, as already recorded.

Commander Norman D. Holbrook V.C., R.N. farms in Sussex. He has a herd of pedigree Guernsey cattle, a beautiful garden and remains an enthusiastic fisherman. Rear-Admiral Edward Courtney Boyle V.C. lives in Berkshire. Though now in his eightieth year, he plays golf on one of our most famous courses. Admiral Sir Martin Dunbar-Nasmith V.C., K.C.B., K.C.M.G., D.L. lives in Morayshire. He has, as ever, many interests, public and private. Forestry is high on the list and he is an enthusiastic carpenter, with a workshop full of cunning personal devices which remind one of his time in E 11. Lieutenant Commander P. S. W. Roberts V.C., D.S.C. has recently retired from the Royal Navy and lives in Devon. Mr. T. W. Gould V.C., lives in London and is the Chief Personnel Officer of one of our great businesses. Rear-Admiral Sir Anthony C. C. Miers V.C., K.B.E., C.B., D.S.O. retired from the Royal Navy in 1959, and is attacking civilian life with his usual gusto. He lives in London. Commander Donald Cameron V.C., transferred to the Royal Navy after the war and continued to serve in submarines until his death in 1961—a great loss to the Service. Captain B. C. G. Place V.C., D.S.C., R.N. is still serving. After the war he volunteered for flying duties and qualified as a pilot. In mid-1962 he was commanding H.M.S. *Rothesay*. He lives in Dorset. Lieutenant Commander I. E. Fraser, V.C., D.S.C., R.N.R. lives in Lancashire. He is the Managing Director of a salvage firm where his knowledge of underwater work is most useful. Mr. J. J. Magennis V.C. lives in Yorkshire and is a radio engineer.

With the coming of the atomic submarine this Branch of the Royal Navy is entering a new phase. Weapons, in our age, change very rapidly. The submarine, of major importance in two World Wars, has had a much longer run than most and is very far from being obsolete. Whatever the future may hold one thing is certain. The precept and example of the fourteen submariners awarded Britain's highest honour will continue to guide and inspire those who go under the sea in ships.

Ham, Wiltshire.   June, 1962.

BIBLIOGRAPHY

ADMIRALTY, NAVAL STAFF: Report of the Committee appointed to Investigate the Attacks Delivered on the Enemy Defences of the Dardanelles Straits (H.M.S.O. 1919)

ADMIRALTY, LORD COMMISSIONER OF: *The Black Sea Pilot* (Eyre & Spottiswoode (for the Hydrographic Office), 1908)

BAXTER, RICHARD: *Stand by to Surface* (Cassell, 1944)

BENSON, JAMES & C. E. T. WARREN: *Above Us the Waves* (George G. Harrap, 1953)

BRODIE, C. G.: *Forlorn Hope 1915* (Frederick Books, 1956)

CARR, WILLIAM: *By Guess and By God* (Hutchinson, 1930)

CHATTERTON, E. KEBLE: *Dardanelles Dilemma* (Rich & Cowan)

CORBETT, SIR JULIAN S.: *Naval Operations* Vols. II & III (Longmans, Green 1920, 1921)

CREAGH, SIR O'MOORE, V.C. and E. M. HUMPHRIES: *The V.C. and D.S.O.* (The Standard Art Book Co. 1924)

CRISMAN, HERMAN HENRY: *Naval Operations in the Mediterranean during the Great War, 1914-1918* (Dissertation submitted to the Department of History of Stamford University, U.S.A. 1931)

EDWARDS, LIEUTENANT COMMANDER KENNETH: *We Dive at Dawn* (Rich & Cowen 1939)

EINSTEIN, LEWIS DAVID: *Inside Constantinople* (E. P. Dutton 1917)

FRASER, IAN: *Frogman V.C.* (Angus & Robertson 1957)

FROST, H. H.: *The Attack on Zeebrugge* (United States Naval Institute Proceedings, March 1929)

FYFE, HERBERT C.: *Submarine Warfare* (Grant Richards 1902)

GUEPRATTE, VICE ADMIRAL P. E.: *L'Expedition des Dardanelles* (Payot Paris 1935)

HART, SYDNEY: *Discharged Dead* (Odhams Press 1956)

HART, SYDNEY: *Submarine 'Upholder'* (Oldbourne Book Co. 1960)

H.M.S.O.: *His Majesty's Submarines* (1945)

H.M.S.O.: *Supplement to the London Gazette*, No. 38204 (Tuesday 10th February, 1948)

KEMP, LIEUTENANT COMMANDER P. K.: *H.M. Submarines* (Herbert Jenkins 1952)

207

KEYES, VICE ADMIRAL SIR ROGER : *Ostend and Zeebrugge Despatches.* Edited by C. Sanford Terry (Oxford University Press, 1919)

KEYES, ADMIRAL OF THE FLEET SIR ROGER : *Naval Memoirs 1916-1918* (Thorton Butterworth 1935)

KEYES, ADMIRAL OF THE FLEET SIR ROGER : *The Fight for Gallipoli* (Eyre & Spottiswoods 1941)

LIPSCOMBE, COMMANDER F. W.: *The British Submarine* (Adam & Charles Black 1954)

MARS, ALISTAIR : *Unbroken* (Frederick Muller 1953)

NEWBOLT, HENRY: *Submarine and Anti-Submarine* (Longmans, Green 1961)

NEWBOLT, HENRY: *Naval Operations.* Vol. IV (Longmans, Green 1923)

ROSKILL, CAPTAIN S. W.: *The War at Sea.* Vols. I & II (H.M.S.O. 1956 & 1961)

Royal United Service Institute Journal, No. 450, LXIII, May, 1918 *The War. Its Naval Side*

HARE-SCOTT, KENNETH : *For Valour* (Peter Garnett 1949)

STEWART, MAJOR RUPERT: *The Book of the Victoria Cross* (Hugh Rees 1916)

STOKER, COMMANDER H. G.: *Straws in the Wind* (Herbert Jenkins 1925)

THOMAZI, A.: *La Guerre Navale aux Dardanelles* (Payor, Paris, 1926)

TURNER, JOHN F.: *V.C.'s of the Royal Navy* (George G. Harrap 1956)

TURNER, JOHN F.: *Periscope Patrol* (George G. Harrap)

USBORNE, VICE ADMIRAL C. V.: *Smoke on the Horizon* (Hodder & Stoughton 1933)

Victoria Cross Centenary Exhibition 1956 Catalogue (Hazell, Watson & Viney)

WESTER-WEMYSS, ADMIRAL OF THE FLEET LORD, K.C.B.: *The Navy in the Dardanelles Campaign* (Hodder & Stoughton 1924)

WILKINS, P. A.: *The History of the Victoria Cross* (Constable 1904)

WILKINSON, COMMANDER BURKE U.S.N.: *Tirpitz Tale* (United States Naval Institute Proceedings Vol. 80 April 1954)

WILKINSON, COMMANDER BURKE U.S.N.: *By Sea and By Stealth* (Peter Davies 1957)

YOUNG, LIEUTENANT COMMANDER E. HILTON R.N.V.R.: (Cornhill Magazine Dec. 1918)

La Guèrre Racontée par Nos Amiraux (Librairie Schwarz, Paris, 1926/27)